Help Yourself to Health

*A Practical Guide
to Spiritual Principles that
Bring Healing and Wholeness*

Charles Sibthorpe

New Wine Press

New Wine Press
PO Box 17
Chichester
West Sussex P020 6YB
England

ISBN: 1 874367 31 0

Typeset by CRB (Drayton) Typesetting Services, Norwich.
Printed in England by Clays Ltd, St Ives plc.

Contents

Acknowledgements

I want to express my thanks to those who have helped in the production of this book. In particular to Alison Kember who has smoothed out my English, untangled my logic and made many helpful contributions. Also, to Monica King and Julian Perkins who have worked on the corrections and the word processing.

Foreword

The other day I met a mutual friend of Charles Sibthorpe and myself. He is getting on in years and I remarked how sprightly and well he looked. With refreshing candour he instantly replied: 'It's the eternal life, you know!' For a moment I was taken aback until I realised the truth of what he had just said. He didn't mean that he was going to live this present life for ever. Christians, like the rest of humanity, are prone to mortality. There are, however, principles of spiritual life offered to us through the Spirit of God which greatly affect the quality and nature of our life here below. I am glad to commend this book to you because it is about these principles of eternal life.

For me the great strength of this little book is the way in which three elements continually interweave; Scripture, testimony and insight. As I read it I felt refreshed and encouraged. More and more these days I am seeing that the principles of the life of faith are not complex or mysterious. They are based on our communion with a God who keeps His word and who has our best at heart.

It is my privilege to have known Charles and Joyce Sibthorpe for a good many years both as friends and fellow workers in the Kingdom, and so I know that the teaching of this book reflects the integrity of their own life and ministry together. I like the way Charles continually relates to the Scriptures, a fact which I know reflects something of his own background and pilgrimage. I especially like the way he has provided a reference at the end of each chapter of all the Scriptures referred to. This will be of invaluable help to those who want to take the study further at a personal level.

The strength of this book does not lie in its novelty. It does not provide that. Rather it provides a clear and uplifting reiteration of vital and life-giving spiritual principles which, if we take them and apply them for ourselves, will release in us the power of life eternal. All in all the book lives up well to its longer sub-title: 'A Practical Guide to Spiritual Principles that bring Healing and Wholeness'.

Bob Gordon
May 1994

Chapter 1

Do not be Wise in your own Eyes

Taking Physical Responsibility

Whilst taking a conference in Eastern Germany, a married couple came to me for prayer and counsel. As we faced one another I enquired why they had asked to see me. We'll call them Klaus and Helga (not their real names).

Klaus spoke first.

'Would you pray for my wife's healing?'

Germans have a amazing way of coming straight to the point.

'Yes, I would be glad to,' I replied, 'what's the problem?'

Klaus turned toward his wife so that she could explain.

'I've got real problems with my feet and ankles; there is constant pain and swelling. I believe that God can heal me.'

'I know that God is able to heal you,' I replied, seeking to bring immediate encouragement and stimulate faith. But one look at Helga quickly revealed the probable reason for her problem; she was grossly overweight.

But, how do you tell a lady that she is too heavy and ought to go on a diet? I hastily looked for words that would be direct yet tactful. As nothing came readily to mind, I decided to ask a question.

'No doubt you've been praying about this swelling in your feet and ankles; has God been speaking to you in any way? Has He given you any reason why your healing has been delayed?'

'No,' she said, 'I can't think why I should have this pain and swelling, or why it has not responded to prayer.'

What do I say now? I thought desperately; I will have to come clean.

'Don't you think that your overweight might have something to do with it?' I said boldly.

'It might do,' came the rather weak response, 'but you see I have six small children and at meal times it is very difficult. I often find myself finishing up the children's leftovers.'

I felt a very real sympathy with her as we have five children and I could remember those times with all the children around the table, when the little scraps seemed so appetizing at the end of the meal!

'God can heal you,' I continued, 'and I am very happy to pray for you and trust that the Lord will heal you in answer to my prayer today. However, I can't promise you that you'll keep your healing if you don't lose the extra weight that you're carrying around, because you are in fact misusing your body.'

I did not feel that my words were getting a very warm reception, but having begun I was bold to continue.

'God is gracious and powerful; He is the mighty healer. But He isn't merely there to deliver you from problems of your own making. As a believer *'your body is a temple of the Holy Spirit, who is in you, whom you have received from God.'* [1] This means that you have a responsibility to look after your body and to be careful how you live. If you ignore and disregard these things you will become vulnerable to sickness; physical, emotional and mental.'

I could see that my words were getting through to both Klaus and Helga, and as we continued to talk together Helga acknowledged that she had allowed her eating habits to become sloppy and her weight had gone totally out of control.

'I think it is about time we prayed,' I said, and laid my

hands on her feet and ankles and asked God's healing power to come.

I can't tell you the end of their story, because I returned to England shortly after this and haven't met them since. But I have recounted this incident because it illustrates a principle.

Taking Spiritual Responsibility

It's not just physical problems that can stand in the way of healing. I think back to one day when the doorbell rang, and there on our doorstep stood Alan looking somewhat forlorn and downcast.

'Come in,' I said ushering him into our lounge where Joyce and I were sitting enjoying a cup of coffee after our evening meal; 'Whatever is the matter with you?'

'Why doesn't God heal me?' The question tumbled out with both anger and perplexity. 'You know that I've been asking God to heal my stammer ever since I became a Christian, why doesn't He do it? I've told God that I want to give my whole life to serve Him and to preach the gospel, but it will be no good if I'm not able to speak fluently and without this stammer. Will you pray for me?'

I knew that Alan had already received prayer on several occasions from people with anointed healing ministries, and so I paused before replying. However, it was Joyce who spoke first; she had been speaking with Alan about a week before and knew things of which I was unaware.

'What about that unforgiveness that we were talking about last week; have you done anything about it yet?' she asked.

'What has that to do with my healing?' Alan retorted; 'If God will heal me of my stammer, I promise Him that everything else in my life will then be put right.'

It was now my turn to jump into the conversation.

'You can't dictate terms to God.' I said, 'Now what's this about unforgiveness; who are you having difficulty in forgiving?'

9

The pain on Alan's face showed me that we had touched a raw spot in his life. Joyce quickly filled in the details. Alan had experienced a very difficult childhood, his parents were now divorced, and in early childhood he had lived with constant rows and even physical abuse. His relationship with his father had completely broken down and he was living with a great mountain of hurt, resentment and bitterness.

Alan couldn't contain himself any longer. 'He doesn't deserve to be forgiven, I can't forgive him, that would be letting him off too lightly.'

'Hang on a minute. Calm down,' I interjected. 'Let me explain something to you, Alan. If you want to receive things from God you need to receive them God's way. It's all here in the Bible, the best healing book that has ever been written. God has His order and priorities. Jesus said, *"If you forgive men when they sin against you, your heavenly Father will also forgive you. But if you do not forgive men their sins, your Father will not forgive you your sins."*[2] When you add to this what is written in the Psalms, *"If I had cherished sin in my heart, the Lord would not have listened,"*[3] you'll realise that God can't respond to your healing prayer while you are holding on to unforgiveness.'

The light was dawning, even though the anger had not yet fully died. I realised that we needed some quality time together when this whole area of unforgiveness could be prayed through carefully and thoroughly.

Later we spent time with Alan doing just that and asking for the Lord's healing power to come into his life. We also dealt with all the hurt and rejection that had been the result of his early childhood.

There are many people who are asking God for healing in their bodies, minds and spirits and wondering why nothing seems to happen. The reason is that spiritually they are living in an unhealthy way, just as Helga was physically unhealthy in her life style.

The Bible describes many ways that healing can come. By the laying on of hands; by a gift of the Holy Spirit; by the intercession of others; by calling the elders and receiving the anointing of oil; by speaking to the mountain; by responding in faith to a word of knowledge or by the power of the presence of God when His people are worshipping.

Many books have been written to teach us how to receive healing through the ways mentioned above, but that is not the purpose of this book. I have said in my first story that Helga had a responsibility to look after her own body and to be careful how she lived. Responsibility is a mark of growth and maturity; it isn't something we expect to find in a child. There can be areas in all of us where we are really still children. Yet it is God's will that each of us should grow to the stature of the fullness of Christ, and be perfect as He is perfect; which means whole, rounded, mature and complete.

You Can Choose!

Moses challenged the children of Israel: *'Now choose life, so that you and your children may live and that you may love the Lord your God, listen to his voice, and hold fast to him. For the Lord is your life, and he will give you many years in the land...'*[4]

The children of Israel had a choice: life and blessing or death and a curse. Eve had a choice. When the serpent tempted her, she could have believed in God's wisdom and goodwill towards her, and refused to doubt Him. Instead she allowed herself to be deceived, and fell. Immediately after the Fall, we find her husband Adam blaming her and her blaming the serpent; both ducking the responsibility. But they had to live with the consequences of their own sin. Eve thought she could choose for herself; what she did not realise was that choosing wrongly had its consequences. By using her God-given free will she had played into the hand of Satan and come under his control.

When Jesus died on the cross, He made it possible for those of us who have received His new life to use our free will to bring ourselves back under God's authority with all the benefits that will result. God's word says, *'Do not be wise in your own eyes; fear the Lord and shun evil. This will bring health to your body and nourishment to your bones.'*[5] We have a choice, and choosing rightly will bring health.

How do we get healthy? We fear the Lord. We set Him above all else in our lives, and study His Word and live by its principles. How do we stay healthy? Exactly the same way. I have found by practical experience that it is easier to stay healthy than to get healed. If you live according to the principles laid down in God's Word, you do not need to get sick; but if you do, you will be half way towards your healing even before you have prayed a healing prayer.

So this book is intended to set out the principles that are laid down in God's word, which, if we live by them, will place us in the pathway of His blessing and in the best possible position to receive the answers to our prayers. Most of the examples given relate to physical healing, but the principles can equally well apply to any situations that need to be transformed by God's power, whether they are physical, emotional, financial, a family situation or a practical area of life.

I have deliberately kept the book short and punchy to make it easy to read; but I do suggest that you take time to digest each chapter, and use the questions at the end of it as a check list for healthy spiritual living.

References

1. 1 Corinthians 6:19
2. Matthew 6:14 & 15
3. Psalm 66:18
4. Deuteronomy 30:19 & 20
5. Proverbs 3:7 & 8

Chapter 2

Have you Asked?

It was a Sunday Evening Celebration and the worship group led by Michael and Ulrike had taken us into the presence of God, producing a great sense of joy and expectancy. It was the perfect preparation for bringing God's word to the people; faith was riding high. I can't remember what I preached about; I can only remember the atmosphere and God's tangible presence. At the end of the service I began praying for people who had various needs. There were those who were committing their lives to Jesus for the first time. It is always a great joy to see people being born again and coming into the Kingdom of God; there is no greater miracle than the miracle of salvation. The fact that we can be forgiven our sins, made righteous and become children of God is always amazing.

I prayed for people to be filled with the Holy Spirit and then finally began praying for those who needed physical healing. Towards the end of this time, I saw Michael and Ulrike walking out to the front of the church. They knelt down together and I knew why they were there, but I also knew that it was costly and humbling for them to come and kneel at the front of their own church. Michael was the son of the Pastor and led both the young people's work and the worship group. They had been married for several years and longed to have children; extensive medical tests had shown that this was very unlikely, perhaps impossible. But with God nothing is impossible! They had consistently testified

13

to their confidence in a God of miracles and that they knew He could give them the child for which they longed. I prayed with them and asked God for a miracle. Time went by and they held on in faith knowing that God would give them the desire of their hearts. He has answered their prayer and now they have two beautiful daughters and a son.

It is great to know that our God is a miracle-working God who loves to hear and answer the prayers of His children. How then are we to receive the answers to our prayers?

You Have to Ask

First of all we need to **ask** in humility and faith as Michael and Ulrike did! That may surprise you. Many times people say, 'God knows my need and if He wants to heal me I know He can.' Unfortunately that kind of statement will do you no good, because Jesus said, *'Until now you have not asked for anything in my name. Ask and you will receive, and your joy will be complete.'* [1]

Asking can be a very humbling experience because we are admitting a need and acknowledging our total inability to be able to do anything about it. Yet humility often opens the door to receiving the healing we are seeking.

It is so important to ask. Many times I have been suffering with something fairly minor like a headache, and have been walking around feeling rather sorry for myself; even telling people how ill I feel. If someone might suggest praying for me, my immediate reaction is to say. 'No, I'll manage, it's just a headache.' Eventually it becomes so painful that I am ready to bury my pride and ask someone to pray for me. On most occasions, within minutes my headache is gone and I'm feeling fine!

Who are you Asking?

Secondly – Who are you asking? Jesus is the healer and when we pray in His Name, we are bringing our need to Him, so that we might experience His mighty power.

King Asa was one of the great kings of the Old Testament and yet at the end of his life when he was afflicted with a disease of the feet he displeased God because he did not seek help from the Lord, but only from the physicians. It was not that God was against the doctors, but He wants His people to always have their eyes upon Him.[2]

I believe that God is saying to each one of us, as He did to King Asa, 'Do you really need me, or am I simply the insurance policy when everything else has been tried and failed?' Have you ever heard someone say, 'We've been to all the doctors and the consultants and they say everything is hopeless, the only thing we can do now is to pray.' No wonder that there is so little success in that kind of praying, because there is so little faith.

I am not against doctors or the medical profession; nor was Jesus, the early Church or the apostle Paul. Luke was known as the beloved physician, a title of affection and honour. And the advances in medical science have helped greatly in making us more healthy and strong. So how do we honour God and use the medical services rightly?

Faith and your Doctor

In our family life we have always worked in this way. First we pray; then, if there has not been an immediate healing, or we do not know what is wrong, we go to the doctor.

Once we have received the diagnosis, we then ask the Lord in which way He wants us to receive healing. Sometimes we have the assurance that it is in God's hands and that He is going to give us our complete healing by His power. At other times we accept the treatment prescribed by the doctor, still keeping our eyes on God who is always the one who brings healing. In any case, doctors can only work with the healing process that has been miraculously placed into our bodies by God.

Always bear in mind though, that doctors have to protect themselves by warning you what might happen; and many have no idea of the hope that only Christ can give you. You need to guard yourself against accepting into your heart the less optimistic statements they make. Doctors themselves have found that the positive, optimistic and cheerful patient is the one who fights illness best. You can be honest in expressing your faith in God whilst still maintaining a relationship of trust between yourself and the doctor, which is very important.

There are, however, medical alternatives being offered these days, such as hypnotism and homeopathy, which are looking to sources other than God for their power. Before accepting any medical treatment make sure that its effectiveness does not come from a power source that is contrary to God.

Your Health Check-Up

● To whom are you looking for your healing?
● Have you asked God to heal you?
● Should you be consulting your doctor?
● Is any of the medical treatment you are receiving emanating from a power source other than God?

References
1. John 16:24
2. 2 Chronicles 16:12

Chapter 3

Will your God Answer your Prayers?

What's your God Like?

What kind of picture of God do you have? Is He a good God who is longing to give you good things? Or is He waiting to pounce on your smallest mistake and punish you? Some folk believe that God puts sickness and disease on people, as a penalty, to teach them a lesson, or perhaps to refine their character. This is such a common belief that it needs some careful attention before we move on.

It is true that those who are experiencing suffering, and turn to God in their time of need, do learn more of His grace and are strengthened in spirit. God will always bring good out of any situation, if He is given the freedom to do so. But it saddens me to see people triumphing **in** sickness when they could be triumphing **over** it and putting it behind them. God sets our spiritual development higher than anything else in our lives, but He does not bring sickness upon us in order to achieve it.

Those of us who have children will always want to see our own children well and happy. Of course, we know they need to learn how to deal with opposition and difficulties in order to develop and mature. However, we would never choose to lead them into trouble, nor leave them in distress any longer than is absolutely necessary; even though we know it isn't always right to whisk them too quickly out of the consequences of their own folly. Why do we suppose God's heart is harder and less loving than ours?

In some cases, if we are honest, difficult circumstances that we're facing have developed out of our own past actions or attitudes. If we can recognise the root of our distress and come to God in repentance, He will show us the way out. Sometimes we carry what I call 'emotional shrapnel' around, hidden inside us. The pressure of circumstances opens up the way for God to ease the shrapnel up to the surface where it can be seen. As we choose to allow Him to remove it and heal us, we can deal with the circumstances and move on.

Incidentally, the Lord gave a friend of mine a revelation that Christ wasn't just wounded that we could be healed; He also carries the scars of His suffering so that we don't need to keep our scars. So don't listen if someone tells you that you'll have to live with emotional damage. God can heal scars, and He wants to do so if you'll let Him.

So the Lord wants to do so much more than support us through our troubles. If we have a fixed idea that He doesn't want to heal us – or that He might want to heal us, but He wants us to suffer first – then we will find it hard to believe that He even wants us to ask, much less that He wants to heal us; and we probably won't get our answer.

What Does the Bible Say?

Let's see what the Bible says. If we look honestly and without preconceptions at the way God develops His relationship with His people from the beginning, we see that the covenants and promises He offers His people are always to bless them, to prosper them, to keep them in safety and in health, as long as they live in obedience and therefore in harmony with Him. Yes, there would be opposition; but they would always overcome when they relied on Him, and achieve victory and peace. The Hebrew word for peace is *shalom*, which expresses the very widest sense of wholeness and harmony as well as an absence of strife and worry. I found this interpretation of *shalom* recently – it means completeness, wholeness, peace, welfare, safety, soundness, tranquillity, prosperity, fullness, rest, harmony; the absence of agitation or discord.

In Deuteronomy,[1] God pronounces the blessings that flow from the obedience of His people as an encouragement to them to follow hard after Him. He also lists the curses as a warning, in advance, to the people and their future generations of what they would bring upon themselves by disobedience. Whenever God's people had good leaders who sought the Lord, they prospered. Whenever they turned away, they lost God's protection and suffered the consequences.

Isaiah gives us this prophecy, *'the punishment that brought us peace* [shalom] *was upon him, and by his wounds we are healed.'*[2] In the New Testament the Greek word used for salvation (*soteria*), like *shalom*, is a far fuller word than the English equivalent. It means deliverance, preservation, soundness, prosperity, happiness, rescue, and general well-being.

God is on your Side

It is important that we understand that evil, sickness and disease is the result of Adam and Eve's sin, when they yielded to the temptation of Satan disguised as a serpent in the Garden of Eden. And what was the real temptation? Not the fruit, wonderful though it must have been. No; the serpent suggested that God wanted to deprive Eve of something good. And she let herself doubt God's goodness, instead of sticking to her faith in God; and she fell.

The wars, famine and catastrophic events that are taking place around the world now are not God's doing. If we think so, we are in danger of committing Eve's sin. The whole world has been thrown out of joint by mankind's sin, encouraged and motivated by the devil.

To quote an old friend of mine, I believe that God is a good God, and the devil is a bad devil. The Bible says, *'The Lord is faithful to all his promises and loving towards all he has made.'*[3] God is on our side, *'If God is for us, who can be against us?'*[4] Jesus said, *'And I will do whatever you ask in my name, so that the Son may bring glory to the Father.'*[5]

Someone I knew was given a little four phrase confession to repeat and build into her spirit: **God is on my side; He is within me; I am safe in Him; Glory be to God.** I suggest you repeat those phrases out loud **now**, and think carefully on each. They are four simple statements that counteract so much wrong thinking.

The Bible says that *'he who doubts is like a wave of the sea, blown and tossed by the wind. That man should not think that he will receive anything from the Lord; he is a double minded man... '*[6] These are severe words, but we should not shrink from them or be crushed by them. But we need to check out how we really see God, because our doubts and fears in the face of troubles may come from messages that have been written on our hearts, unseen by us.

Family Portraits of God

Your experience of your own family will have a direct bearing on how you think of God, even though you may not be aware of it on the surface. Did you have a loving and forgiving father? Did he respond readily and generously to your requests? Or was he hard, mean and always looking for opportunities to put you down and to punish you for the smallest mistake?

Your secret heart will see God in the same way as you saw your father, and this can mean that you are divided in yourself between the mind – which reads the Word and gives it willing assent – and your secret heart which doubts it. Such hidden doubts sometimes surface in surprising ways.

I well remember an incident from my own childhood. On Saturdays I usually went to my grandmother's house and played with my cousin Tim. He lived in a flat in the same house with his mother; his father having died as a prisoner of war during the Second World War. Saturday was the day when our grandmother cooked a chicken dinner, which was a very special treat, in the days when a chicken was a rare delicacy. At one o'clock precisely we would arrive in the dining room with hands and faces scrubbed clean from the morning's exploits, ready for the feast.

On one particular day, as I was waiting for my grandmother to arrive through the door and show us to our chairs, I happened to count up the number of places set at the large mahogany table and to my horror, it seemed that there was one place missing. I immediately presumed that I had not been expected, and rather than suffer the pain of rejection and banishment from the meal table, I slipped away unnoticed and sped home on my bicycle. As I entered the door, I saw my mother, telephone in hand, talking to a puzzled grandmother who was enquiring as to the whereabouts of her missing grandson. My calculations had been wrong, I was expected all along, it only remained for my tears to be wiped away by my mother and for me to return to the banquet.

It isn't a conscious sin to have misunderstandings of God in your heart; don't feel crushed by guilt if you find them inside you. But they can make a hidden barrier between you and God which will have hampered your progress, and you need to consciously repent of them and detach your image of God from the image of your father or your family. Choose to see God as He really is, and assert that truth over the past experiences that have deceived you.

Are you in God's Family?

Do you ever remember being asked by a friend from school to join the family on a day out? Of course you knew your friend very well because you were at school together, but you were unfamiliar with the rest of the family. Do you remember the point when ice creams were being bought for the family? That moment of anxiety; would you be included in the treat, or would you be left out? Do you remember the joy of being included, of receiving a large ice cream cone, and even getting it before your friend? Or were you left out and had to buy your own?

So then, will God answer your prayers or leave you to manage on your own? Yes, His promise is to answer the prayers of His children. It is important that you know that you are a child of God, which comes by receiving a new birth and a new life from Jesus. Most of those reading this book will have already come to a living faith in Jesus. If you do not have the assurance that you are a child of God, you can pray this prayer now and if you mean it in your heart, as well as saying it with your mouth, God will give you His new life today.

> Father, I acknowledge that I need the new life and salvation that comes only through what Jesus did for me on the cross.
> I confess that my old life has led me away from You into sin.
> I repent of that life of sin and ask You to forgive and receive me.
> I believe that through the blood of Jesus I will receive forgiveness and new life; that I will be saved from the old life and be born anew into Your life.
> I invite You to come into my life, to be the Lord and to take authority and control of my life by the power of Your Holy Spirit.
> I now know that I have become Your child and that You love me and will care for me for the rest of my life.
> I thank You for hearing me and receiving me and coming to live within me.
> I pray this in the Name of the Lord Jesus. Amen.

You are now adopted into God's family and therefore inherit all the rights and privileges of a child of God. The

Bible uses a phrase to describe this; it says that you are *'in Christ'*[7] which means that God will do for you the same as He will do for His own Son Jesus. He loves you like His own Son; Jesus confirmed this when He said, *'As the Father has loved me, so have I loved you.'*[8]

Don't Blame God

However, if you are already in God's family and you have still been waiting for a long time to receive the answer to your prayer, it is very easy to get discouraged, to lapse into unbelief, or even to blame God for your situation. This is very serious and you need to repent, because if you blame Him you cut yourself off from His love and power. Paul says to Timothy, *'If we died with him, we will also live with him; if we endure, we will also reign with him; **if we disown him, he will also disown us**; if we are faithless, he will remain faithful, for he cannot disown himself.'*[9]

Isaiah says, *'Yet the Lord longs to be gracious to you; he rises to show you compassion.'*[10]

Remember, as you wait expectantly for your miracle, the words that are written about Jesus which say, *'For we do not have a high priest who is unable to sympathise with our weaknesses, but we have one who has been tempted in every way, just as we are – yet was without sin. Let us then approach the throne of grace with confidence, so that we may receive mercy and find grace to help us in our time of need.'*[11]

Your Health Check-Up

- Do you believe that God is a good God and wants the very best for you?
- Do you believe God wants to answer your prayers?
- Have you grieved God by blaming Him for your sickness or problem?
- Do you acknowledge that the problems of this world are the result of sin and the activity of Satan?

References

1. Deuteronomy 28
2. Isaiah 53:5
3. Psalm 145:13
4. Romans 8:31
5. John 14:13
6. James 1:6–8
7. 1 Corinthians 1:30
8. John 15:9
9. 2 Timothy 2:11–13
10. Isaiah 30:18
11. Hebrews 4:15–16

Chapter 4

Are you a Worshipper?

Worship can Heal

Some time ago I heard of a man, Stewart Duke, who was crippled as the result of a stroke. His arm, his leg and his speech were all severely affected. To this had been added the shattering blow of losing his wife through the after effects of an accident. His life became a nightmare of struggling with loneliness and immobility. Some of his friends suggested that a dog would be company for him. They even told him of a breeder down on the coast at Rye who had two or three pups available. But what was the use? It was all he could do to get himself out and down the steps from his flat, and even worse to get himself back up again. How could he ever cope with a dog with its needs and walks?

Stewart came to a meeting where Ian Andrews was ministering. He was preaching from Proverbs 30:18 & 19 about the eagle which crouches high up on a rock, listening for the sound of a rising current of air. He likened that picture of the eagle to the members of God's family listening for the wind of the Spirit of God. I will now quote from the account given in Ian's book, *God Can Do It For You* (Nelson Word 1982).

'When that wind current comes,' Ian explained, 'all you need to do is soar up with praise and worship into the presence of God.' He turned to look around the crowded hall.

'When the wind of the Spirit is here, as I believe it is now, Ian continued, 'you can get as close to God as you want to if you let your spirits rise with His Spirit.'

'I suggest everybody present seeks to rise now in praise and worship – you can be healed in this way, you can be baptised in the Holy Spirit as you rise in the presence of God.'

Stewart had never heard anything like it before but he let himself reach out and respond and was filled with a feeling of elation.

Ian never did go on to the rest of his talk. The Spirit of God took over the meeting and Stewart was only one of the many who was affected deep down in his being.

The meeting eventually ended and Stewart made his way to the door.

'Would you like me to walk you home?' It was his Catholic friend alongside him in the crowd.

'No thank you very much. No. I shall be quite alright.' Somehow it seemed unnecessary. He got outside without a problem and then, still elated and thinking about the service he walked home and up the stairs to his flat. Then it dawned on him. He hadn't had to rest all the way home! And, incredibly, he had walked straight up twenty-eight stairs without a stop. It must be the result of the great elation that made him still feel like that eagle soaring up in the sky.

Stewart went to bed relaxed, elated, the best he had felt for ages. He eagerly looked forward to being in church the next morning. Then, as he lay there feeling wonderful and thinking over all that had taken place that evening, a gentle voice seemed to say to him, 'Go and get that dog.' Get that dog, he thought. What an extraordinary thought to break in on the wonder he felt at his experience in the meeting. But there it was again, 'Go and get that dog.' Would God tell him something like that? It seemed such a silly thing even to think, but, over and over again he heard, 'Go and get that dog.'

Lying in bed thinking, thinking, thinking, Stewart

remembered the way he strode home just like old times. He thought of the way he strode straight up those twenty-eight stairs. Dare he believe that God had touched him and restored the ravages of the stroke of two years before? If He had, then maybe he could after all look after a little dog.

It was Sunday when Stewart woke up so he had his bath and dressed for church. And it was true! His leg was restored. His arm was as good as new, and when he spoke to himself in the mirror, there was no slurring, no mumbling, he could speak clearly again. He could hardly wait to meet his friend at church and tell him what God had done for him.

Then, there it was again, right out of the blue and totally unexpected, 'Go and get that dog.' Well, he would. He would do just that. With a feeling of suppressed excitement, he packed up some sandwiches for himself, collected a few biscuits and a container of water for the pup, put some money in his pocket and he was off down the stairs.

With great thankfulness welling up within him he knew with every step that God loved him, Stewart Duke. God had healed him. Here he was getting into his car to drive without a problem all the way to Rye and back when twenty four hours before he had wondered whether he should try to drive any distance at all in his state.

On returning home with a delightful little black Scottie, the first thing on the agenda was a good sharp walk right around a local grassy area. What joy and gratitude he felt on finding it presented no problem at all!

That's an amazing and true story of how God's power was received by one who discovered the potential of being a worshipper of God in spirit and truth. It illustrates an important principle – worshipping the living God is a doorway into the healing and wholeness of God.

God said to the Israelites in the desert, *'Worship the Lord your God, and his blessing will be on your food and water. I will take away sickness from among you, and none will miscarry or be barren in your land. I will give you a full life span.'*[1]

What does it mean to be a worshipper? Well, it is not simply singing songs in church or attending services of worship. King David said in one of his psalms, *'Praise the Lord, O my soul; all my inmost being praise his holy Name.'*[2] Again in another psalm, *'My heart and my flesh cry out for the living God.'*[3]

IT IS singing, praising, dancing, rejoicing and being joyful in the Lord. **BUT** more than that, it is a heart attitude towards God; making Him the focus and whole direction of your life.

Here is a very important fact. You will never rise higher than the object of your worship! Think about it. Your whole life will revolve around that object of worship. It might be your career, hobby or sport, it could be a member of your family. If your whole life is centred around television, for example, it simply means that you worship television, and your life will rise no higher than the concepts and philosophies that are shown on the screen. There are even people whose whole lives are focused upon their sickness, which means that they worship sickness. It is no surprise, then, that they are perpetually ill.

Raising Hands in Worship

I believe that raising hands in worship is a very powerful thing. It therefore does not surprise me that I initially found it so difficult.

My debut in this field of spiritual experience was at the Capel Bible Week some years ago. I had been baptised in the Holy Spirit for about a year, and this was the first time I had experienced joyful exuberant worship. As everyone else was praising the Lord with freedom and abandonment it seemed that someone had hung 25kg weights on each of my wrists! I wondered why it was so difficult; I just longed to be able to do what seemed so easy to everyone else. I knew that it had not been part of the tradition of my church, but it was in the Bible. As the days went by my frustration increased; the only consolation being that my wife Joyce seemed to be experiencing the same difficulties. All too quickly we had arrived at the final service and I could sense that this was my last chance. The time of worship was underway and I could feel the Lord's presence all around. As the opportunity threatened to slip by, I summoned all my will power and managed to raise one hand in the air. I began at shoulder level, then as my courage increased I lifted it fully up. The higher it went the more free I felt. It seemed that a power which had been holding me back was broken.

Was there a power holding me back? Yes, I believe that the enemy knows the force that is released when we obey God's Word. This power is one reason why I believe that it remains an area of spiritual battle. The devil fears the people of God with hands raised in worship to Him. I believe that they signify something deeper than merely following a modern or ancient trend.

Hands up! What's Happening?

A couple of years ago whilst taking a Church Weekend in Slough, the Lord spoke to me about what is happening when we raise our hands to Him in our worship. During that service, as my colleague David was leading worship from the piano, a tremendous anointing fell upon the meeting, the singing moved from song to song and the presence of God was tangible. There was no way that it was right to stop this at the end of the normally allotted time, so I let it continue. As time passed, the message that I had prepared to preach became totally inappropriate. It was at this moment that the Lord suddenly showed me five things that are happening when we raise hands to Him in praise, adoration and worship. This I was to use later as my sermon!

First, think of one of those Westerns that you have seen on television. The saloon is full of cowboys; suddenly the door swings open and in walks John Wayne with his six-shooter at the ready. 'Hands Up!' he snaps, and suddenly the whole atmosphere changes as he takes control. God does not put a gun to our heads, but when we raise our hands in worship we are symbolising an act of surrender which is an important aspect of worship. There is no threat. We yield out of love not fear. We are saying – 'I surrender, You are the Lord, You are in control, You have the right to rule in my life.'

Secondly, I was reminded of the time when our children were very young. Each day I would leave the house to go to my work in the family department store; in the evening I would return home. As I walked in through the door I would call out to let everyone know that I was back. It was always a great thrill to have one of my children come running with arms in the air, wanting me to pick them up and give them a cuddle. What they were saying with their actions was – 'Daddy, I love you, I need you, it's lovely to have you back home and to be near you.' Is that not what we are saying as we reach out our arms to the Lord in worship?

Thirdly, as our hands are raised we are saying symbolically, 'Jesus, we lift You up, we give You the highest place.' The words of one of our most anointed worship songs says, 'Jesus we enthrone You, We proclaim You our King, Standing here in the midst of us, We raise You up with our praise. And as we worship, build Your throne ... Come Lord Jesus and take Your place.'[4]

Jesus Himself said, *'But I, when I am lifted up from the earth, will draw all men to myself.'*[5] When we lift Jesus to the highest place we are in a wonderful position to receive from Him.

Fourthly, I was shown that when our hands are raised in the air they are empty hands. We cannot hold on to anything and at the same time hold them high above our heads. In Paul's letter to Timothy he writes, *'I want men everywhere to lift up holy hands in prayer, without anger or disputing.'*[6] When hands are raised to God in this way I believe that it is impossible to continue holding on to resentment and bitterness. This openness of heart and spirit unlocks a way for God to pour out upon us His blessings and answers to our prayers.

Lastly, as we hold our hands in the air they form the shape of a funnel. We are symbolically saying, 'Fill me Lord with more of your Holy Spirit, I need your power, I cannot live my life in my own strength, fill me again and again.'

A Song in the Morning

Let me ask you what you do the moment you wake up in the morning. Do you worry over the details of the day? Do you let all the burdens of life weigh you down? Or do you sing praises to God?

I have discovered that the moment of waking up is a time of extreme vulnerability. You have a choice. You can allow the anxieties, burdens and demands of the day to fill your heart and mind, and weigh you down with concern and even fear, or you can tune into heaven and fill your heart and voice with the praises of God. I call it singing a 'Song in the Morning'.

I know this has transformed the lives of many people. It is a very important part of my own walk with God. He will give you a song each day if you will meet three conditions. First, you need to ask God to give you a song of praise to sing to Him at the start of each day. That is no great problem, because Jesus said, *'Ask and it will be given to you.'*[7]

Secondly, the moment you awake you need to listen carefully for the song that God is giving. You don't need to worry, for He never fails. Radio Heaven is broadcasting the praises of God 24 hours a day, and you are simply 'tuning in'!

Thirdly, you need to sing the song that you are given and the others that will follow. For if you do not act upon what you are given, you will not continue to receive. How loud you sing your song depends upon your own living situation. It does not need to wake the neighbours, or the children, to bring joy to God and to set your day on course for victory.

31

Eyes only for Him

I once heard the American Bible Teacher, Judson Cornwall tell this story. Some years ago, a stray dog turned up at his home and just kept hanging around the property. He tried to persuade it to find its own home, but as it kept coming back, he realised that it needed feeding, which with a certain reluctance he did, knowing it would encourage the dog to stay. As the days went by, in his mind he determined to take it to the home for stray dogs; but each time he was about to take decisive action, two large soft brown eyes burrowed into his heart, and he gave it some more food. He resolved, nevertheless, that it was not going to be admitted to the family home; it could live outside in the back yard. However, every time Judson returned home two large brown eyes would fix on him longingly, pleading for an entrance into the house. Judson's resolve weakened and it was not long before the dog gained admission into the home and into the hearts of the family. Now, whenever Judson was at home, and in the same room as the dog, those two large soft brown eyes were fixed upon him. It did not matter who else was in that room, this dog had eyes only for Judson. I think that is a wonderful picture of adoration, which is an aspect of our worship. We have a God who has rescued us from hopelessness and despair; do we have eyes only for him? In the letter to the Hebrews it says, *'Let us fix our eyes on Jesus, the author and perfecter of our faith.'*[8]

If your whole life is filled with worship, praise and adoration, you will be in the very best position to receive the answers to your prayers, and to be in the flow of God's purposes and blessing.

Your Health Check-Up

- Is your life focused upon the living God in love and worship?
- Are you looking to Him in every situation?

- Are you drawing your strength from Him?
- Is your life fully submitted to God?

References

1. Exodus 23:25
2. Psalm 103:1
3. Psalm 84:2
4. Written by Paul Kyle. Copyright © 1980 Thankyou Music, PO Box 75, Eastbourne BN23 6NW
5 John 12:32
6. 1 Timothy 2:8
7. Matthew 7:7
8. Hebrews 12:2

Chapter 5

Are you Thankful?

Eat a Thanksgiving Sandwich!

The noises coming from the transmission of my car told me that all was not well. A visit to the garage confirmed my worst suspicions, and when the estimate arrived my misery was complete. The repair was going to cost me £600 which I did not have; to continue to use the car would only make matters worse. So I took it to the garage, left it there and rode home on my son's bicycle, feeling totally downcast.

Everyone who came to our house or spoke to me on the phone was subjected to my tale of woe. A cloud of gloom came down over our home. Anyone who spoke to me about anything got their head bitten off! Several days went by and all attempts to lift my spirits failed.

One morning a few days later I woke up quite early and went downstairs to pray, or to be more accurate, to have a good moan to the Lord. As I was thinking about my problem and wondering how I was going to find the money to redeem my car from the garage, I heard a voice inside me say, 'Eat a thanksgiving sandwich!'

'Whatever is that?' I thought to myself; but as I pondered the truth began to dawn.

As you well know, a sandwich is made up of two pieces of bread with a filling in the middle. The Lord showed me that the top piece of bread in this sandwich was praise and worship. I needed to exalt the Name of the Lord, to worship and honour Him especially at this time of difficulty. As we have seen in the last chapter, worship establishes the throne of God in our hearts and shows us His greatness and ability. This has the effect of dethroning all other gods, especially those of fear, doubt and discouragement. As I praised God I could feel my anxiety and despair subsiding, and the peace of God filling my heart.

Now I was coming to the filling, which always gives the name to the sandwich – hence Thanksgiving. Paul's instructions to the Philippians were, *'Do not be anxious about anything, but in everything, by prayer and petition, with thanksgiving, present your requests to God.'*[1]

As I began looking back over the months and years, I was simply overwhelmed by the goodness of God. We had looked to God for all our financial provision for more than 16 years and He had never let us down. We had seen His care and protection for our five children for more than 25 years. God had never failed, He had not made any mistakes in my life, and He was not about to begin now. My heart began to overflow with thanksgiving to my faithful and unchangeable God. Confidence was restored and my faith was rising.

Now it was time for some more praise – the lower piece of bread in the sandwich. I began to celebrate and rejoice because I was about to see God do a miracle. Paul wrote to the Corinthians, *'For no matter how many promises God has made, they are "Yes" in Christ. And so through him the "Amen" is spoken by us to the glory of God.'*[2] Praise declares the faithfulness of God, and speaks of His ability to meet our needs. I also believe that praise speeds up the answer to our prayers, because it keeps us in a place of faith and expectancy.

Thanksgiving is so often a sacrifice, because it is costly to do it in the face of adverse circumstances. In the Psalms it says, *'He who sacrifices thank offerings honours me, and he prepares the way so that I may show him the salvation of God.'*[3] I picture thank offerings as a highway that is being constructed by our thanksgivings and which is the road God can use to bring an answer to our prayers.

By the time the family appeared for breakfast, I was a different person, which brought a great sense of relief all round. I now knew that I could trust God to release the money that was needed to pay for the car repair. Day by day I continued to thank God for the answer to my prayer.

Within a couple of days I had to leave for a ministry trip in Germany and so left Joyce at the sharp end of the faith battle. Just two days before the car was due for collection the phone rang in our home and there was a friend on the other end.

'Do you have a particular need at this moment, because God seems to be directing us to send you quite a large gift?'

I don't have to tell you the reply that Joyce gave; you will have already guessed.

The following day a cheque arrived in the post for exactly £600! And Joyce had not even told them the amount required. It was now her turn to climb on Craig's bike and, carrying a bundle of money, to go and redeem the car with great joy and praises to God.

Stress, Anxiety and Worry: the Antidote

Stress, anxiety and worry are the cause of a great deal of sickness and disease. The Bible tells us that we can live free from worry and anxiety and that thanksgiving is the key. There was a time when I was constantly plagued with anxieties, until a friend said to me one day, 'You can either pray or you can worry, you can't do both.' This just about blew my mind, as I thought that worry was a fact of life, experienced by everyone and something that one just got used to living with. I had become accustomed to that dull ache in the pit of the stomach which was a constant reminder of all the worries that I carried around daily. In fact, if at any time the pain disappeared, I got worried because there was nothing to worry about. I even felt that not being anxious about a problem was being irresponsible!

Then my friend explained; 'You have a choice; you can carry your burdens or you can give them to Jesus, it's as easy as that.' Peter says it in his letter, *'Cast all your anxiety on him because he cares for you.'*[4] It's very simple really, but it only works if you do it.

Paul's instructions to the Philippians are a step by step guide to gaining complete victory over worry and anxiety: *'Do not be anxious about anything, but in everything, by prayer and petition, with thanksgiving, present your requests to God.'*[5] Those are the instructions, and the promise follows: *'And the peace of God, which transcends all understanding, will guard your hearts and minds in Christ Jesus.'*[6]

'Do not be anxious about anything' is a command which I suppose in today's colloquial English would be, 'Don't worry!' The only reason it is stated in the Bible so simply is that it is possible for everyone, but only if you take note of the following points.

'But in everything' means everything. It is often easier to bring the big problems and worries to Jesus than the little ones which we like to keep to ourselves. The Word says *'everything'* and that is what it means. *'By prayer and petition'* – be specific, vague prayers get vague answers, specific prayers receive specific answers.

'With thanksgiving' – here is the key phrase. To pray with thanksgiving means that as you bring your specific 'need of the moment' to God, you look back to situations in the past where you received answers to prayer, and where you experienced God lifting your anxiety and giving you His peace. This assures you of His faithfulness. As you ask Him to help you now you thank Him for meeting your needs in the past. 'Lord, you did it then, you can do it again!' This will quell your doubts and increase your faith, and this is vital because without faith you will not receive the answer to your prayer.

Now, here comes the promise: *'And the peace of God which transcends all understanding'* – it is not a natural peace, it is a supernatural peace, because it *'will guard your heart and mind in Christ Jesus.'* Your heart will be at peace, which means the knot in your stomach will disappear. Your mind will stop churning over all the problems and difficulties which are the root of your anxiety, and you will be bathed in a serenity that can only come from the heart of God. (A further development of the battle between fear and peace is given in Chapter 8.)

I often tell a story that my father frequently used in his preaching. There was a poor man who had gone to the market to buy a sack of potatoes. Having made his purchase, he was slowly walking home burdened with the heavy load on his back, when a neighbouring farmer drew alongside in a horse and cart. 'Can I give you a lift home, those potatoes look very heavy?' came the invitation. The poor man gratefully climbed onto the cart and the journey continued. After a few moments the farmer looked around to see the poor man still carrying the potatoes on his back. 'Put your load down, man,' said the farmer speaking with kindness yet authority. To which the poor man replied, 'It is very kind of you to give **me** a lift home, I wouldn't expect you to carry the potatoes as well.'

This story never fails to bring smiles to people's faces whenever I tell it. Our laughter indicates we are identifying with the story. Yes, we all know that we can so easily carry burdens that Jesus would lift from our shoulders if only we would let Him.

Your Health Check-Up

- Are you thanking God for His greatness and His ability to answer all your prayers?
- Are you declaring that God knows what He is doing and that it is for your good and not evil?
- Are you thanking God for all the ways He has answered your prayers in the past?
- Are you thanking God that He is now meeting your present needs?

References

1. Philippians 4:6
2. 2 Corinthians 1:20
3. Psalm 50:23
4. 1 Peter 5:7
5. Philippians 4:6
6. Philippians 4:7

Chapter 6

Are you a Forgiver?

Unforgiveness is Torment

For eight years we worked with Colin Urquhart and the Bethany Fellowship, now known as Kingdom Faith Ministries. The work was then based on a large country house called The Hyde in Sussex and we lived in one of the cottages in the grounds. It was quite usual for young people to come from abroad and to work in the fellowship for periods of up to a year, so that they could live in an environment of faith and also improve their English.

Brigitte, from West Germany, was an attractive girl in her late teens, who came for six months before commencing her training as a nurse. She lived in our household as part of our family and her daily work was in our Resources Centre where we sent out a Bible Teaching Course on cassette and other items requested from our Mail Order Catalogue.

She seemed to be well adjusted having been brought up in a Christian home. However, we very quickly realised that she had great problems with unforgiveness.

Each day Brigitte would be picked up and taken by car to the office a few miles away from The Hyde, where she would spend her working day with other members of the Fellowship before returning in the evening. To be able to understand fully the problems that confronted Brigitte you need to understand something of the German character and their culture. German people are known for their punctuality and politeness, which is where the difficulties began. To start with, her transport to the office was provided by Brian whose punctuality was not good. Work was due to commence at 9 a.m. and it was often as much as ten past nine before the car drew up outside our house; which did not provide a good start to the day for Brigitte. What followed only made matters worse, because upon arrival at the office, rather than being greeted individually by each of her workmates with the customary German handshake, all she received was the general English/American greeting 'Hi!'

What this communicated to Brigitte was a deep sense of rejection, and her response was one of unforgiveness. Part of the problem was cultural, some of it was Brian's bad timekeeping. But the real problem lay in Brigitte's reaction; it led to a deep resentment of the way she felt she was being treated, which meant that by the time she returned home in the evening she seemed to be moving under a black thunder cloud. She would often come into the house complaining of a migraine headache and disappear to her bedroom saying that she did not want anything to eat. The gloom would slowly descend upon the whole house.

Moodiness, sulking and isolation are something that has never been tolerated in our home, and Brigitte had come to be part of the family. So one day Joyce went upstairs to her room to try and find out the cause of the latest crisis.

'What happened today at the office?' was the opening question.

'Nothing, I've got a headache and I'm just not feeling well,' came the sullen reply.

'When did your headache begin?' Joyce continued.

'I have had it since this morning,' Brigitte said gloomily. It was hard work getting any response at all.

'Has anyone upset you at work;' the probing continued, 'is there someone who you need to forgive?'

'Forgive! I can't forgive them, they will only do it again and I don't feel like forgiving anyway.'

The words began to tumble out as her anger and

frustration were vented. 'Brian was late picking me up this morning, in fact I thought he had forgotten me altogether, he probably doesn't even care about it. Then, when we arrived at the office the others couldn't even bother to say good morning properly. By that time my headache had already begun and I have been sad and miserable all day. All I want to do now is to go to bed. I will probably feel better in the morning.'

'But you need to forgive.' Joyce was insistent.

'I can't.'

'Forgiveness is not a feeling, it is an act of your will. You need to do it because God tells you to in His Word, and you will not have any peace until you do.'

'I won't forgive them, they don't deserve it and they will probably do it again.'

'You didn't deserve the forgiveness that Jesus gave you when you became a Christian; they may possibly do it again, but that is no reason for not forgiving.' Joyce was not going to be deterred in her mission.

'Jesus told a parable to show how important it is to live in forgiveness,' she continued, 'it was about a king who had a servant who owed him an enormous sum of money; in present day values it would probably be about £5,000,000. This the servant was totally unable to pay, and he fell upon his knees before the king to ask for mercy. The king took pity on him and cancelled the debt. As the servant was going on his way he met a fellow-servant who owed him about £50. He demanded it back, but his colleague was unable to pay and asked for time and patience. He totally refused to show any leniency and had the man thrown into prison. When the king discovered this he was very angry, withdrew his act of kindness, and handed the servant over to the jailers to be tortured.' [1]

'This isn't just a dramatic story. It illustrates a vital spiritual principle. When someone won't extend forgiveness to another, even though God has forgiven him for so much, the effect is to leave that unforgiving person in a state of torment. It sounds rather horrific but that is what happens,' Joyce explained carefully.

Brigitte was startled; 'Do you think that is the reason why I often get a severe headache when these upsets happen?'

'I'm sure of it,' was the instant reply.

At this point Joyce was able to lead Brigitte to pray and to forgive all those who had hurt and offended her during that day. It was not many minutes before she appeared downstairs to say that the headache had now gone and to ask whether there was any food!

As they talked together later that evening, Brigitte explained how every time there was an upset in her family, she had run away to her room refusing to forgive. At times she would experience headaches but she had never before connected these with the unforgiveness. Joyce was able to explain that Jesus had placed forgiveness at the centre of His teaching because unless we learn to forgive we cannot receive forgiveness from the Lord.

As the weeks went by Brigitte began to learn this principle and to put it into practice in her life. It wasn't always easy because old habits can be difficult to break. However, once she had grasped the truth of God's Word she knew that it was the only way to live. It was also the end of the migraine headaches!

Unforgiveness is Sin

Unforgiveness is sin, not only towards those who have offended you, but also toward anyone whom you have offended and with whom you have not sought any reconciliation. If you hold on to sin in your life God is not able to answer your prayers; remember it says in the Psalms, *'If I had cherished sin in my heart, the Lord would not have listened.'*[2]

Personal guilt can also be a form of unforgiveness. Even though we know that God has forgiven us our sins because of the cleansing blood of Jesus, if we are not able to forgive ourselves we will still feel guilty. This too will hinder our prayers and any work of healing that we may be needing in our lives.

Isaiah the prophet says of God; *'You have put all my sins behind your back.'*[3] He not only puts our sins out of sight; he also puts them out of reach, *'As far as the east is from the west, so far has he removed our transgressions from us;'*[4] out of mind, *'For I will forgive their wickedness and will remember their sins no more;'*[5] and out of existence, *'I have swept away your offences like a cloud, your sins like a morning mist.'*[6] When we have been forgiven we need to let this truth set us free from our feelings of self-blame.

It is possible to become involved in the arguments and conflicts of others and start taking sides. This too is a form of unforgiveness and can become very negative, leading to critical attitudes and a spirit of judgement. It is possible to become so taken up with such a situation of conflict that you can become even more distressed than those who are directly involved. Your role in these situations is to pray and not participate in the sin of others.

Choose to Forgive

A friend of mine has a principle by which he lives daily. He says, 'I choose not to be offended by anyone, but I choose to forgive everyone, no matter what they do to me.' To follow this example means you have to learn to respond with immediate forgiveness, not instant offence and anger. An example that I have found people understand most readily, is a practice of Colin Urquhart's. If he is travelling in the car and some other vehicle cuts in dangerously causing heavy braking or other avoiding action, Colin has learned to say at that moment; 'I forgive you!' The tension is broken, anger subsides and peace is restored.

Blaming God

There is one further form of unforgiveness that may lie unnoticed in our hearts for years. I met someone once who had been born with a birth defect, which necessitated repeated surgery in early life. Nevertheless he became a Christian, married, had children (who were free from the defect) and felt he had left all the hurt of the past behind him. Then one day he found himself facing the trauma of going back into hospital for minor surgery, and realised just how terrified he was at the prospect. Quite unreasonably terrified, it seemed, for he had forgotten his childhood experiences until they came rising uncontrolled to the surface. He came across Psalm 139:13–14 *'For you created my inmost being; you knit me together in my mother's womb. I praise you because I am fearfully and wonderfully made...'*

Up came a surge of rage and bitterness he'd not known was hidden inside him. How could God have *'knit him together'* and got it so wrong? How could He have done this to him? What had he ever done, an innocent embryo, to deserve that defect and the suffering it had brought him? He raged and wept for an hour or more.

Finally he stopped to listen and hear what God had to say. God said, very quietly: 'What a lot you hold against me. Do you forgive me?'

Of course, he knew in his head that God hadn't really offended against him; the defect and the sorrow it had brought weren't God's deliberate doing, they were the result of the imperfect and fallen world in which he had been formed and into which he had been born. Yet his heart must have blamed God deep inside. God didn't need his forgiveness, God had done nothing wrong. Yet he knew he needed to forgive God. He had to set himself free from that old unseen sin. In so doing, he was healed of so much that had affected him for years.

So we may need to check out whether we are knowingly or unconsciously blaming God for something. If we are, we are sinning against Him and we need to get it sorted out.

In my experience of ministry, which goes back for many years, I have found that unforgiveness is the biggest single barrier to receiving freedom and deliverance from God, and also to receiving answers to prayer.

Your Health Check-Up

- Is there anyone either alive or dead who you have not forgiven?
- Are you making it a principle in your life to forgive everybody at all times?
- Have you forgiven yourself for everything that has happened in your life, because if you have received Jesus as the Lord of your life, He has forgiven you?
- Have you become involved with the conflicts of others? If so, you need to turn your judgement into prayer and release the situation into the hands of God.
- Have you blamed God for anything that has happened to you in the past? Even if you've stopped blaming Him now, have you gone back to that sin and repented of it and released yourself from it?

References

1. Matthew 18:21–35
2. Psalm 66:18
3. Isaiah 38:17
4. Psalm 103:12
5. Jeremiah 31:34
6. Isaiah 44:22

Chapter 7

Are you a Giver?

Jesus said, *'Give and it will be given to you.'*[1] Giving has always been a spiritual principle in both the new and old covenants, and it doesn't simply mean giving money.

Looking Outwards: Giving in Prayer

I remember being very impressed when I first heard the testimony of Pastor John Osteen's wife Dodie who experienced a remarkable healing from cancer. John Osteen is the Pastor of Lakewood Church, in Houston, Texas. The doctors had given Dodie three weeks to live; there was nothing more – either medically or surgically – that could be done to combat the virulent liver cancer that raged in her body.

Dodie discharged herself from hospital and went home. She and John fell on their faces and cried out to God for His healing power and grace. They took hold of God's Word and began to confess that what God declared was more powerful than the cancer, the diagnosis of the doctor, or the attack of the devil.

It was not a quick and easy healing, it was a battle against the disease, fear and the enemy. One thing God taught Dodie was that even at the height of the battle she still needed to be a giver. She constantly prayed for the sick even when she felt so ill she would rather have been in bed.

She also continued to care for and minister to the needs of her family. It was deliberate giving to fulfil this principle.

The battle raged for more than two years, but at the end of that time the doctor's diagnosis showed no trace of cancer left in her body. It is more than ten years since Dodie received her miracle and she continues to be actively involved in ministry with John at Lakewood Church.

When we are in the middle of a faith battle, one of the chief things that the enemy tries to throw at us is discouragement. If we take it on board, it soon leads us to self-pity, which is a very destructive force. It makes us look at others and become jealous of all their blessings, it feeds doubt in our minds and undermines faith; and we begin to question God. The way to avoid this descending spiral is to look outwards and give to others.

Several years ago I had an idea to grow more vegetables in my garden. It seemed a good economy to be able to have free food from the garden as the price of everything was constantly rising. In order to extend the vegetable patch I needed to dig up part of the lawn, which was going to be hard work. I therefore decided to hire a cultivator to make the job easier and more efficient.

In order to get the best value for money, I set aside a day for the project, and arrived at the hire shop early in the morning, so that the moment it opened I could pick up the machine. I drove home quickly and applied myself diligently to the task. I worked right through the day producing a beautiful piece of well tilled soil, which I was sure would produce a bountiful crop. Just before the hire shop closed I returned the cultivator and arrived home satisfied with a job well done.

Once my fatigue had subsided, I discovered a legacy of the day's endeavour. I had injured my elbow; the straight lifting movements were not too difficult, but a rotating motion was extremely painful. I was reminded of this injury daily, as I made the early morning cup of tea. Lifting up the tea pot and pouring the tea into the cups was almost impossible.

So, I began to pray for healing; laid my hand on the elbow proclaiming the healing power of Jesus. I rebuked the pain and told it to leave my body; I commanded strength to return and everything to go back to normal. I did everything I had ever been taught about healing. Nothing worked. Every morning I would have a fresh reminder of my unhealed elbow!

After a few weeks I realised that this elbow was beginning to dominate my thoughts and was really getting me down. I made a conscious decision that I was going to forget about it and just get on with living normally.

Several weeks went by, and I was beginning to learn to live with the pain and discomfort. Then, one evening while we were having our home Bible Study group a young man asked me to pray for him. He had a back problem and wanted me to lay my hands on him and pray for his healing, which I was glad to do. The power of God came on him and soon he was rejoicing in his healing.

The next morning, when I went downstairs to make the customary cup of tea, to my surprise and delight I discovered that my elbow was healed. Praise the Lord! As I began to think about it, I reasoned that as I had laid my hands on my friend, and the power of God had come through me and onto him, it must have healed me on the way down! The Bible says that a man reaps what he sows; *'Let us not become weary in doing good, for at the proper time we will reap a harvest if we do not give up.'*[2] God's principles work!

Giving Money

I believe that our lack of giving prevents God giving back to us so many things that we desire. It is vital, for instance, that we are obedient in giving to God financially. Tithing (or giving one tenth of your income to God) was the law under the old covenant, so it should be the minimum we give under the new covenant! Whenever God's people failed to fulfil their obligation in tithing they suffered. In

Malachi, God challenges the people to bring the whole tithe into the storehouse, and then He says, *'Test me in this, and see if I will not throw open the floodgates of heaven and pour out so much blessing that you will not have enough room for it.'*[3]

In fact Jesus himself confirmed the principle of tithing in His teaching in the gospels where He says, *'Woe to you, teachers of the law and Pharisees, you hypocrites! You give a tenth of your spices – mint, dill and cummin. But you have neglected the more important matters of the law – justice, mercy and faithfulness. You should have practised the latter without neglecting the former.'*[4]

Paul tells the Corinthians, *'Remember this: whoever sows sparingly will also reap sparingly, and whoever sows generously will also reap generously ... for God loves a cheerful giver.'*[5] Later on he adds this, *'You will be made rich in every way so that you can be generous on every occasion.'*[6]

It's not wrong to give expecting to be blessed in return. As we do so, we are attesting to our belief in God's word – which says we will be blessed by His generous and over-flowing kindness. If we treat Him as if He is a mean and grudging God, that's what we will receive. When Jacob met God and received a promise of blessing, he more or less cut it down to, 'I'll serve you if you'll keep me alive;' which wasn't what God had promised. So even though God's blessing followed him, it didn't really benefit him directly – it all went to his Uncle Laban and in the end Jacob had great difficulty in extricating himself from the tangle he landed himself in by limiting what God could do for him. It was only then he was able to enjoy the blessings that had been promised to him for so many years.

God's Word works. I know people who are not even believers, but who put this principle of giving into practice in their lives, and are proving that it works. It says in the Proverbs, *'A generous man will prosper; he who refreshes others will himself be refreshed.'*[7]

Giving is such a central pillar to experiencing the enjoyment of God's blessing and answered prayer. Whenever we have lack or needs in our family Joyce will always ask me, 'Are we up to date with our giving?' Here is another Proverb, *'One man gives freely, yet gains even more; another withholds unduly, but comes to poverty.'*[8]

Giving Love

The principle applies beyond the material realm; if self-pity and discouragement is trying to get a grip, you will find that giving love and care to someone else regardless of your own emotional need will provide the cure. Loneliness is a great problem, not only in today's society but also in the Church. The best way to gain friendship is to give friendship to someone else, not wait until they give to you.

The devil has sown lies into the hearts of people, and says to them, 'You look after yourself, no one else will.' 'You keep what you earn, the tax man takes away enough already.' 'Why spend your time and energy helping others? You will wear yourself out.' 'When God heals you then you will be able to pray for others.'

It is not the truth, and the devil knows it, but he is trying to prevent you enjoying the blessings that come when you obey what God says.

Your Health Check-Up

- Are you a giver, or are you a taker?
- Are you always looking out for opportunities to meet the needs of others through your love, praying and giving?
- Are you robbing God financially?
- Are you sowing your seed, financially, emotionally and in every way possible, and also expecting to receive a good return?
- Is it your aim to refresh those who you meet each day?

References

1. Luke 6:38
2. Galatians 6:9
3. Malachi 3:10
4. Matthew 23:23
5. 2 Corinthians 9:6, 7
6. 2 Corinthians 9:11
7. Proverbs 11:25
8. Proverbs 11:24

Chapter 8

Are you at Peace?

Fear is the Enemy

Baptised in the Holy Spirit at last! All the questions and searching of the past two years had come to an end; for on the previous evening Joyce and I had received the blessing that God, for so long, had desired to pour out upon us. We had asked and received. Why had it seemed so difficult?

That was back in 1969; we had gone with a number of young people to a conference centre in Northern Ireland, and through the ministry of Barry Kissell had been filled with the Holy Spirit. The joy and release was tremendous; the abiding sense of the presence of God in our lives was very real. Yet there seemed to be some unfinished business lurking in the wings.

For, whilst chatting together with the leaders of the centre the following evening, one of them, John, looked directly at Joyce. 'Is there anything wrong? You look anxious about something.'

'I'm anxious and fearful about everything, I always have been,' was Joyce's spontaneous reply.

'That's wrong. You don't need to be dominated by fear. Have you ever asked God to set you free from it?' John spoke kindly and sensitively.

'No. I thought fear was a fact of life that affected some people more than others; once you had it, you were stuck with it,' she continued. 'My mother is full of fear, which she communicated to me as a child, and the whole of my life I've battled with it. To be honest; at the moment, I am feeling very anxious about the safety of our two older children who we have left with friends back in Cornwall. I know it's absolutely irrational, because I trust them completely. They have two children of their own, and I know that Craig and Joanna will be totally safe in their hands.' Joyce was now in full flow. 'This fear is so illogical. I'm afraid of the dark as well. Admittedly, we do live in a very large and rambling house, but when I've been pregnant and want to go to the toilet in the middle of the night, I need to wake Charles to accompany me. He's very patient, but I feel so foolish. There are also times that Charles needs to go away on business, and I'm too afraid to be alone, so we need to find someone to stay with me in the house whilst he is away. But I thought that it was something I'd have to live with for the rest of my life. Is there a way to be free from this fear, and can you help me?' John and the other leaders were quick to give a resounding 'Yes.'

This led to a time of prayer when the power of the enemy was bound, for the devil is the source of this kind of fear, and Joyce was set free. The peace that came upon her was tremendous, and this was followed by some very helpful explanation.

'To understand the character of fear, the simplest way I know is to give you an acrostic on the letters F-E-A-R; False Expectation Appearing Real,' John explained. 'That is what the devil is always trying to do, filling your mind with lies and threatening suggestions, trying to dominate and control your thoughts. What we've done is to bind the power of those fears in you, and we've told them to leave you by the power of the Name of Jesus. It's quite obvious from looking at you that they've gone.'

'Yes, I'm totally at peace; in fact I feel a completely different person,' Joyce was quick to affirm.

'What I need to do now is to teach you how to stay free from fear and counter any further attacks from the enemy.

These will come, because your mind is constantly being filled with thoughts that come from many sources. One of these is the voice of the devil, and he always speaks lies. Jesus said of Satan, *"When he lies, he speaks his native language, for he is a liar and the father of lies.'*[1] Another definition describes him as, *'the thief who comes only to steal and kill and destroy."*[2] You need to learn to distinguish between the many voices that can speak into your mind.'

This was proving to be most valuable. John went on, 'I want you to imagine the situation when you get home. You are now free from fear and you know the words of Paul which he spoke to Timothy, *"For God has not given us a spirit of fear, but of power and of love and of a sound mind."*[3] Now, you wake up in the middle of the night and need to go to the toilet. By the way, you are not expecting another baby, are you?'

'No, certainly not,' Joyce retorted, as three month old Daniel slept peacefully in the carry cot alongside her.

'Forgive my teasing: let's get back to our example,' said John, still smiling at Joyce's reaction to his question. 'You've woken in the night and are about to go to the toilet. Now that you're free from fear you will have no problems with the darkness in the passage outside the bedroom door, will you?' John did not wait for a response from Joyce, but gave his own reply, 'Now the answer to that question may not be a direct **"no"**, because the enemy will want to regain the ground that he has lost. "Nothing's changed," he will try to say, "you're still frightened of the dark, somebody is lurking out there in the gloom waiting to pounce on you." This is where you need to answer him with the word of God, in exactly the same way that Jesus did when He was verbally attacked in the wilderness. You need to confront him by saying, "The Bible says, *'God has not given me a spirit of fear, but he has given me a spirit of power, and of love and of a sound mind.'*[3] Go away Satan, because you are not welcome here!" He must obey, just as he did when Jesus used the Word of God against him. That's the way to counter the lies of the devil.'

This was so helpful to Joyce; because having been bound by fear for such a long time, she needed to learn how to live her new life of freedom and peace.

Maintaining Peace

Peace is such a delicate thing. You know when you have it, and you most certainly know when it has gone. The vital question is how to regain your peace when it escapes. It is also very important to know that the peace that God puts into your heart is not the kind of peace that is talked about in today's society, which is merely an absence of conflict. Jesus said, *'Peace I leave with you; my peace I give you. I do not give to you as the world gives. Do not let your hearts be troubled and do not be afraid.'*[4] This peace is *shalom*; wholeness, health, tranquillity.

Stress, tension and anxiety are the source of most of the illness and disease in today's world. Some months ago, I read a statement made by an eminent doctor, who said that if he could find a cure for anxiety, he could empty the majority of hospital beds in this country. Doctors are also finding that stress reduces the effectiveness of the body's immune system.

True peace does not come because there are no problems or conflicts, but through our knowledge of and faith in a God who is able to deliver us from the problems and resolve the conflicts. We are not only brought to peace with God as we receive forgiveness of sin through Jesus, but we can receive the *'peace of God which transcends all understanding.'*[5] Peace is also part of the fruit of the Spirit and will be in evidence in every Spirit filled life.[6]

Freedom from fear as Joyce experienced it, is available for every believer in Jesus. Over the years, both Joyce and I have prayed with hundreds of people, and rejoiced to see them enter into that same freedom and peace. This is a fundamental 'ground clearing' operation if we are ever to learn to live in daily peace and victory.

Having established that foundation of peace in our

hearts, we need to learn how to maintain it through all the challenges of life. I believe that there are three key things that we need to know and to have as a foundation for our daily peace.

Know that God is Good and has Greater Power than the Devil

We need to believe in our innermost being that God is for us, He is totally committed to us, His power is greater than the devil's, and His plan for us is blessing. As Paul says, *'If God is for us, who can be against us?'*[7] We will then be like one of those children's toy dolls on a spherical base, with a low centre of gravity, that always bounce back no matter how hard you push them over.

This can only come through our personal relationship with God. It takes time and commitment to develop trust. The psalmist says, *'Blessed is the man who fears the Lord, who finds great delight in his commands ... He will have no fear of bad news; his heart is steadfast, trusting in the Lord.'*[8] The shocks of the world won't knock him off balance.

He wants you to be as carefree as a little child. Our grand-daughter Gillian is 2½ years old; the trust and confidence that she demonstrates in those she loves is incredible. There is no expectancy that anyone will harm her; and when she leaps from our staircase into the air, she has total confidence that she will fall safely into the arms below. *'You will keep in perfect peace him whose mind is steadfast, because he trusts in you,'*[9] are the words of the prophet Isaiah.

Consistent reading of, and meditating on the Word of God, the Bible, is essential for maintaining a place of peace. A verse from the Psalms says this, *'Great peace have they who love your law, and nothing can make them stumble.'*[10]

This is one of the reasons I published the *Workman's Bible Reading Plans*. I wanted to help and encourage people to read the whole Bible regularly and consistently. They are available and can enable you to read the Bible right through in One or Two years. There are details at the back of this book to tell you how to obtain these booklets.

When the 72 disciples returned from their mission, Jesus spoke these words to them, *'I have given you authority to trample on snakes and scorpions and to overcome all the power of the enemy; nothing will harm you.'*[11] Jesus had given them His authority over the power of Satan, which is now extended to all who have committed their lives to Jesus and who live under His Lordship.

Balaam had been hired by King Balak to curse the Children of Israel; but God would not let him, and he found himself pronouncing blessings and saying, *'God is not a man that he should lie, nor a son of man that he should change his mind. Does he speak and then not act? Does he promise and not fulfil? I have received a command to bless: he has blessed and I cannot change it.'*[12] Those words were true when spoken by Balaam thousands of years ago, and they have not changed today. God has blessed you in Christ, and that blessing stands.

Learn to Recognise the Voices you Hear

Your peace will depend entirely upon your state of mind. It is important, therefore, to know the source of your thoughts and so to be able to deal with those which rob you of that peace.

All thought will have its source. Most of the time we think our own thoughts, but as these are a mixture of all the experiences of our life to date, they will come in all shapes and sizes. They will be moulded by our family and upbringing, they will reflect our education and social class, and be influenced on a day-to-day basis by the stimulus of our friends, work and the things we hear and see on radio and TV. If we are believers in Jesus and regularly spend time in worship, reading God's Word and prayer, that will have a profound and beneficial effect on our thought life.

Lastly, the devil is involved, as he is constantly trying to dominate and control the minds of the human race.

Learning to listen to God is one of the most creative ways of counteracting the lies of the enemy. God wants to speak to all His children; for Jesus said, *'He who belongs to God hears what God says.'*[13] I am always surprised to discover the many Christians who are not confident in hearing God. There is not space here to give such teaching, so if you are one of those who is insecure in this area, I suggest you find some teaching on the subject and learn how to tune in to the Almighty. At the back of this book you will find details of how you can obtain a Cassette Teaching Set by my wife Joyce entitled *Developing Spiritual Sensitivity* which gives specific and helpful teaching on how to hear God.

Our children's exploits, as they grew up and began to extend their wings, were often a source of enemy attack. Fear could very easily creep in when they were out with friends or abroad on their adventures. One day Joyce came across a verse in Proverbs that has been a great strength and defence against the suggestions of the enemy. It says, *'Whoever listens to me will live in safety and be at ease, without fear of harm.'*[14] We have put this into practice and taught it to our children, and it has worked.

When you have learned to recognise the voice of God, and you are becoming more familiar with the Bible, you will know when your thoughts are in harmony with God. However, thoughts which come from your upbringing which are negative and disturbing need to be dealt with, so that they do not rob you of the peace which you have received from God. This is why we need to –

Take Every Thought Captive

For those who have put their faith in God, Paul says, *'For though we live in the world, we do not wage war as the world does. The weapons we fight with are not the weapons of the world. On the contrary, they have divine power to demolish strongholds. We demolish arguments and every pretension that sets itself up against the knowledge of God, and we take captive every thought to make it obedient to Christ.'* [15] It is so important to be able to demolish the arguments in the mind. When a negative thought enters our mind, the devil seeks to use that thought to disturb our peace and ultimately to destroy us.

Develop a strategy to counteract these thoughts. When you have a disagreement with another person, refuse to enter into mental arguments in your own mind. If it is a genuine misunderstanding or you have been offended, you must go to the person and seek forgiveness and reconciliation. When you have forgiven, forget the grievance, don't ever mention it to anyone again.

Don't listen to doom-mongers and gloomy predictions or imagine scenarios of future disaster. Don't keep on telling others of the deprivations and misfortunes of your past. Forgive and forget.

It is possible to allow your mind to become a 'devil's playground' by permitting all sorts of rubbish to rule unchecked in your brain. That is why Paul warns the Romans, *'Do not let the world around you squeeze you into its mould, but be transformed by the renewing of your mind. Then you will be able to test and approve what God's will is – his good, pleasing and perfect will.'* [16] The apostle John at the very end of his life wrote these words, *'Jesus who was born of God keeps the believer from the relentless temptation and snare of the wicked one.'* [17]

If we desire to be in the right state to receive the healing power of God into every area of our lives, it is vital that we learn to maintain and establish a foundation of peace in our lives.

Your Health Check-Up

- Have you recognised and been set free from all the fears in your past?
- Are you confident that God's hand is upon you for blessing and not cursing?

- Are you learning to recognise the source of all thoughts that rob you of peace, and taking the appropriate action?
- Are you protecting your mind, by filling your thoughts with God's Word, and the assurance of His faithfulness?

References

1. John 8:44
2. John 10:10
3. 2 Timothy 1:7 (NKJV)
4. John 14:27
5. Philippians 4:7
6. Galatians 5:22
7. Romans 8:31
8. Psalm 112:1 & 7
9. Isaiah 26:3
10. Psalm 119:165
11. Luke 10:19
12. Numbers 23:19 & 20
13. John 8:47
14. Proverbs 1:33
15. 2 Corinthians 10:3–5
16. Romans 12:2 (partly from J.B. Phillips paraphrase)
17. 1 John 5:18 (Margin translation NKJV)

Chapter 9

What are you Saying?

Confess with your Mouth

Jim had been a churchgoer all his life; it was not until an evangelist came to his local church for a special weekend of meetings that he realised that he had not received Jesus into his life, and therefore had not been born again. He listened intently to the preaching and realised his need for a personal encounter with Christ. At the close of the service he responded to the invitation, and spoke with the preacher, who prayed with him.

By the time they had finished talking together everyone else had left the church and Margaret, Jim's wife, was waiting for him in their car. The journey home was in silence, Margaret seeming reluctant to ask Jim the reason for his prolonged conversation with the evangelist. Jim said nothing, but was waiting for some feelings to rise within him, which never came.

The evangelist had clearly explained the way of salvation and shown him the scripture in Romans where it says, *'That if you confess with your mouth, "Jesus is Lord," and believe in your heart that God raised him from the dead, you will be saved. For it is with your heart that you believe and are justified, and it is with your mouth that you confess and are saved.'* [1] They had prayed together and Jim had left. The evangelist fully expected him to tell his wife what had happened, but Jim was waiting for the feelings.

As the days and weeks rolled by Margaret became puzzled about the unexplained conversation between Jim and the evangelist, but she never enquired, and soon it had almost faded from her memory. Jim had not forgotten, he was just confused.

A whole year went by and the evangelist returned for another weekend of outreach at the same church. Jim and Margaret were in their usual places, and at the end of the service Jim stalked out to the front to speak to the preacher. He was angry and confused and his words just tumbled out.

'Last year you prayed with me to become a Christian and to invite Jesus into my life, and it didn't work!'

The evangelist was quick to reply, 'What did you do when you left here last year? Did you speak about your new faith and did you tell your wife?'

'No,' was the curt reply. 'I was waiting to feel different before I said anything.'

'That's your problem, Jim,' the evangelist continued; 'the scripture that I showed you clearly said, *"it is with your heart you believe and are justified and with your mouth you confess and are saved."*[1] You have only fulfilled half of the conditions.'

'You mean to say that because I did not tell my wife or anyone else, Jesus has not given me salvation?' retorted Jim.

'Not exactly, the scripture says that with your heart you believe and are justified. God has done his part and given you his righteousness, but before this can become powerful in your life you must do your part,' the preacher explained. 'Confessing, here, means speaking out with your mouth what you believe in your heart.'

'Will you pray with me again, so that we can do it properly this time?' Jim's question came.

'No! I am not praying with you again, there was nothing wrong with last year's prayer; all you have to do now is to confess that Jesus is your Lord.'

The conversation had taken some time, and once again Margaret was sitting in the car awaiting Jim's arrival. As he climbed behind the wheel Margaret's question just popped out. 'What's been going on with you?'

'One year ago I made Jesus the Lord of my life,' he replied, and immediately burst into tears, as the joy and presence of God swept over him.

Jim had confessed Jesus as Lord and the transaction was complete. Now he was able to enter into the blessing that was rightfully his, because of what was promised in God's Word.

This testimony underlines an important spiritual truth. The promises of God are received in the heart and confessed with the mouth. The words that you say are important! In the book of Proverbs it says, *'The tongue has the power of life and death.'*[2] That's a very strong statement, but it is true.

I heard recently about a concert pianist, who was not a Christian, but had been saying for many years, 'By the time I reach the age of fifty I will have played everything I will ever want to play, and there will be no point in living any more.' Shortly after he became fifty he died. His words which were in effect a curse had come true!

That's an extreme case. But if you sat down, say in a café, for about half an hour and listened to the conversations around you, you would very quickly hear the confession of your neighbours. They would speak about their fears, discouragements and disappointments. You would hear a catalogue of woes and all their aches and pains. Yes, you would hear about the good things in life, but you know and I know that most of what the average person says is very negative, whether they are a Christian or not, particularly in England, where we somehow glory in gloom. But everything we say, positive or negative, agrees with either heaven or hell, success or failure, blessing or cursing. Personally I'd much rather agree with God and strengthen His hold on my life than give the devil a chance! Few people realise that their words have power and can bind them in fear, sickness, weakness and failure.

Jesus said, *'You will know the truth, and the truth will set you free.'*[3] You need to know the truth and to speak the truth. Then it will set you free.

Confess the Word

When we went to join Colin Urquhart and his work at The Hyde, God had been teaching the fellowship about the confession of their mouths. Each person had agreed that they would bring their speech into line with God's word, and we committed ourselves to correct one another when we said the wrong things. We were all horrified with the negativity that had become second nature. It was not an easy task to change a way of speaking that had been ingrained for so many years, but we were surprised at the difference it made.

When someone said, 'I feel so bad, I'm such a sinner, I'm sure God must be very angry with me,' we would say, 'That's not true – you are forgiven, you are righteous, you are accepted in Jesus.'

If the confession was, 'I feel so unworthy, God will never answer my prayers,' the answer was, 'You are a son of God, you are a joint heir with Jesus. Whatever God will do for Jesus He will do for you.'

In the general routine tasks of the day you would hear, 'I can't do that, I know I will make a mess of it and so I would rather not try.' 'Yes you can, because *you can do all things through Christ who gives you strength.'*[4] Let me add here, however, that I do not believe this verse is saying that Christ will enable you to do anything you choose to do. But I do believe that He will enable you to do those things that He has given you to do, or that are part of the general responsibilities and calling on your life.

When there was financial need it was all too easy to say, 'I'm broke, I know I shall never be able to afford to pay for that.' The reply would come, 'Wait a minute; God's Word says, *"My God will meet all your needs according to his glorious riches in Christ Jesus."'* [5]

In times of weakness we learned to say, *'I am strong in the Lord.'* [6] *'The Lord is my rock, my fortress and my deliverer; my God is my rock, in whom I take refuge.'* [7]

As someone might be looking at the coming day with a sense of foreboding, Colin would come through the door saying, 'It's another day of victory in Jesus!' The biblical background for this statement comes from the words Paul spoke to the Corinthians, *'But thanks be to God, who always leads us in triumphal procession in Christ Jesus.'* [8] Jesus wants every day to be a day of victory, because He has won a complete, eternal and irrevocable victory over Satan and provided a way that we can enjoy that triumph in our daily lives.

When sickness would attack we would confess, 'The Lord is my healer, by the stripes of Jesus I am healed,' [9] or 'I reject all these symptoms and tell them to leave my body, because Jesus died to defeat sickness and I declare His Lordship over my body today.'

In times of fear we learned to confess, *'I have not been given a spirit of fear, but a spirit of power and of love and of a sound mind.'* [10]

This may sound artificial at first; which is the impression Joyce and I had when we arrived at The Hyde. The truth spoken boldly even caused some bruised feelings at the beginning. We are told to *'speak the truth in love'*; [11] we had to learn that truth applied to each other should always contain comfort as well as confrontation, encouragement as well as exhortation. Do you remember when you learned to ride a bicycle, or taught someone to ride one? Remember the hand that was needed at the back of the saddle adjusting the balance as you lurched from side to side? If you had not given time and commitment to learn and had that correction, encouragement and comfort, you wouldn't have learned to ride alone, you might still need a parent or energetic friend hanging on the back to keep you on top.

Progress would be wobbly and slow and prone to painful mishaps!

Why did we believe it was so important to speak out God's positive Word in every circumstance? Because we discovered it made a real difference. We believed it was right, we put it into practice and found that it worked. There is a mysterious learning process which happens as we speak words out, hear them with our ears and receive them in our brains. It's as if we are constantly washing the words though our minds, washing good thoughts in and chasing bad ones out. Primary teachers, when I was at school, knew all about this process. Did you have to recite your times tables day after day, until they became automatic? I did.

When you decide that you are going to eliminate negative speech and to speak what is true and positive as each situation arises, a gradual growth and development will take place in your mind and your heart, and you will come to have the conviction that what you are saying is true. What you believe in your heart you must confess with your mouth to be saved. The opposite is also true; what you say with your mouth, you'll come to believe in your heart. By speaking God's word, you are building faith. Wouldn't you rather be believing something good and true than something negative and bad?

As you apply these principles to your life, you discover that speaking the truth has dramatic and life changing effect. Those negative attitudes go, you begin to enjoy a strength and victory in your life that you did not dream was possible. You receive answers to your prayers and achieve an altogether new measure of victory over the attacks of Satan. It's like cycling instead of walking.

Confessing the Truth

Let's be clear about this, though. I am not advocating foolishness. God is a God of wisdom and truth. If you have a lump, or an illness, it is a fact, and hiding from that won't change anything. It only allows fear to germinate and grow in secret, and lumps feed on fear. Your feelings need to be brought to the light and dealt with wisely and constructively.

So what about that stubborn situation that refuses to be changed whatever you do or say? It may be the lump that was mentioned above, or a need in your family or finances. What do you do now? You need to repent of your fear and receive God's peace, then you can ask Him what His purposes are for your situation. You will find His promises in the Bible; get His Word for your situation. Now what do you do? This is where we find the example of Abraham so helpful.

Abram was childless, which was a disgrace and a tragedy in the culture of his day, but he had received a promise from God that he would have a son, and that his descendants would be like the stars in the sky and the sand on the seashore. Years went by and nothing happened; he even made some mistakes trying to speed up God's answer. The Bible tells us that God continued to restate the promise and Abram stuck to his faith. As a confirmation of His good intentions, God even changed his name from Abram to Abraham; his new name meant 'Father of many Nations' in a culture where the meaning of names was very important. As Abraham informed his friends of the change, or corrected them if they used his old name, he was speaking out and confessing the truth of the promise yet unfulfilled.

Abraham's confession is described by Paul as imitating God himself, *'He is our father in the sight of God, in whom he believed – the God who gives life to the dead and calls things that are not as though they were.'*[12]

This isn't God turning a blind eye to things, fooling himself and denying reality. But like Abraham and his God we need to look beyond the present, and call into existence (by what we say) the things that are not yet true in our experience. We are told that Abraham did not consider the seeming physical impossibility that a man of 100 should be able to father a child by his 90 year old wife. *'Yet he did not waver through unbelief regarding the promise of God, but was strengthened in his faith and gave glory to God, being fully persuaded that God had the "power to do what he had promised"'*[13]

So in the face of our need we declare the truth of God's faithfulness, love, power, willingness to heal, and all-sufficiency. The truth of God's Word spoken out loud in words of scripture enables the Lord to establish His reign and Kingdom within us.

Songs of praise can help us to declare the truth; many of these have words that are taken straight from scripture. As we sing them over and over again we will feed our spirits, strengthen our faith, and create an environment where God can work in us releasing His healing and deliverance.

When you are in the middle of a faith battle the words that you speak are vitally important. Your words need to agree with God's Word. You are a new creation in Christ, and everything that He says He has given to you is yours, but you have to lay hold of it with the words of your mouth.

Confessing out Loud

There's another aspect to speaking out the truth. I believe it is important that your confession is made out loud, because I can find no evidence that the devil is a mind reader. We do not have a specific scripture for this, but I do find people attributing the 'all knowing' quality of God also to the devil. I do not believe the devil is going to know your faith in the Word and power of God until you speak it out. When you speak the Word in the face of all the circumstances that surround you, you are releasing God's power. His power will break every force that is trying to bring defeat, fear, sickness or anything else upon you. The Word is the Sword of the Spirit, and will always inflict a defeat upon the enemy.

Smith Wigglesworth was a mighty man of God, under whose ministry occurred some of the most remarkable modern-day miracles. One day, when asked how he was able to live in victory over his emotions and feelings, he replied, 'When I get up in the morning, I don't ask Smith Wigglesworth how he feels. I tell Smith Wigglesworth how he feels!' He had learned the power of confessing the Word.

Your Health Check-Up

- Are your words negative or are they positive?
- Does your speech agree with the Word of God?
- Are you consistently speaking out the truths of God's Word in the face of the circumstances?
- You will see the power of God released into every area of your life where your confession is in line with His promises.

References

1. Romans 10:9, 10
2. Proverbs 18:21
3. John 8:32
4. Philippians 4:13
5. Philippians 4:19
6. Joel 3:10
7. Psalm 18:2
8. 2 Corinthians 2:14
9. Isaiah 53:5
10. 2 Timothy 1:7 (NKJV)
11. Ephesians 4:15
12. Romans 4:17
13. Romans 4:20 & 21

Chapter 10

Who has the Last Word?

It was a November evening and Joyce and I were spending a relaxing time in front of the fire. On the following day I was due to travel to Sweden for two and a half weeks of ministry. I had been aware of some tenderness and discomfort in my testicles for several days; becoming curious I went to the bathroom to investigate further, and to my horror discovered a lump. The first thing that came into my mind was 'cancer'!

Suddenly my mind became a whirl: what should I do? Was this cancer? Should I cancel my trip to Sweden and go to the doctor? Should I tell Joyce? And another hundred questions besides began to crowd my thoughts. 'Keep calm!' I thought to myself, 'don't panic!' So I prayed, 'Lord, what shall I do? Shall I go to Sweden? Shall I cancel the trip and see a doctor? Shall I tell Joyce?' I needed some answers quickly.

The answer I received was swift and strong; I clearly heard the Lord say to me, *'Wist ye not that I must be about my Father's business?'* These were the words that Jesus spoke to His parents after they had been searching for Him and He had remained in the temple in Jerusalem after the passover. Yes, it was right to go to Sweden; I also knew that this was a battle that I would need to fight alone for the time being, because there was no way that I would leave Joyce in a place of potential fear as I flew out.

For the moment I rebuked the lump, commanded it to wither and disperse, and spoke healing into my body. I also took authority over fear and declared that it had no right to dominate my thoughts or emotions. All this had taken place in a few brief moments and I returned to the fireside as if nothing had happened.

Early the next morning I caught the coach to Heathrow, and in the two hours it takes to travel from Bristol to Heathrow Airport I had time to think and pray. My first battle concerned fear and foolishness; was this the most naive and stupid thing I had ever done? With my whole life and health at stake, I was heading towards Sweden to preach and teach.

Immediately I remembered the testimony of Dodie Osteen, which had been one of the most moving and thrilling testimonies of healing that I had ever heard (see Chapter 7). It had not been a quick miracle, but she had taken hold of the Word of God and declared it in the face of all the symptoms, the diagnosis of the doctor, and the attack of the enemy. Dodie's struggle against the killer cancer had lasted for two years, but God won! She did not give up the battle but clung tenaciously to the promises of God, *'for He who promised is faithful.'*[1] Today she is totally healed, a vibrant example of the triumph of faith and courage as she ministers alongside her husband John Osteen.

I had shared Dodie's testimony many times in my preaching, and God had used it to stimulate faith and action in those involved in similar faith battles. It is one thing to preach it; but now it was my turn to put it into practice. It almost seemed foolishness to think that speaking out words from the Bible was going to be more effective than receiving expert medical attention. I was now experiencing for myself the battle that rages in the mind. Pictures came flashing through my brain: Joyce widowed at such an early age; my children fatherless; never being able to see my grandchildren; hospitalisation and surgery; pain and suffering. I took authority over them in Jesus' Name and told them to go! Peace would return for a few hours, until there was a slack moment and they would all come flooding back and the struggle would start over again.

By now I had reached the airport and the routine mechanics of catching my flight to Malmo in the south of Sweden now replaced these thoughts. After an uneventful journey it was good to see the familiar face of Mats as he met me at the airport. I was glad that I had planned to arrive 24 hours before my schedule began, because it would give me time to pray and prepare. By this time it was late, so I was glad to have a comfortable bed to sleep in, and to be able to forget everything for the time being.

As the alarm clock sounded and consciousness was thrust upon me, the stark reality of my situation slowly seeped back into my mind. The lump was still there, and I was far from home and alone with my faith battle. After breakfast I returned to my room. Now was the time to formulate my strategy. I again rebuked the lump commanding it to wither and die, and spoke the healing power of Jesus into my body. I then took hold of my Bible and prayed, 'Lord, will you lead me to those scriptures that are your words for my situation?' I also opened my notebook so that I could write down the verses that God was going to give me.

Immediately words from the Psalms came into my mind; *'I will not die but live, and will proclaim what the Lord has done.'*[2] I wrote them down and spoke them out strongly. I then found myself turning over a few more pages and looking at Psalm 128 where another promise came alive within me. *'Thus is the man blessed who fears the Lord . . . and may you live to see your children's children.'*[3] That's a great promise. Two of our children had been married during the year and as yet there had not been any reports of little ones on the way! But I would live to see my grandchildren.

I turned on to Proverbs to very familiar verses that I had read many times. *'My son, pay attention to what I say; listen closely to my words. Do not let them out of your sight, keep them within your heart, for they are life to those who find them and health to a man's whole body.'*[4]

I wrote the words down in my notebook and began to

declare them, changing the way they were written so that they became my personal testimony. 'Lord, I am paying attention to what you are saying, I am listening closely to your words, I will not let them out of my sight and will keep them in my heart. I thank you that they are the source of my life and they are healing to my whole body.'

Then God led me to Exodus and to the promise that He gave to His people when He said, *'I will give you a full life-span.'*[5] This is getting better all the time, I thought. Then my mind went to another of the Psalms of David, which he wrote when his life was under threat from Saul. *'What gain is there in my destruction, in my going down into the pit? Will the dust praise you? Will it proclaim your faithfulness?'*[6]

David had learned the importance of praising God at all times. He also knew that God needed people who would worship Him, so he argued his case before the Almighty. 'Lord, if you let Saul kill me, who is going to take my place and give you constant praise? Saul won't! Will the dust praise you? You need to keep me alive because I am one of your praising people.' I took up David's argument and began to use it in the same way. I added another verse from Psalm 119 which says, *'Let me live that I may praise you, and may your laws sustain me.'*[7]

This was going well; as I spoke out each scripture my faith rose higher. This is not going to take long I thought. But suddenly I came back to the reality of my situation; I had not come to Sweden for a prolonged prayer meeting about my healing but to fulfil a very demanding itinerary. My conflict of interests was also testing my faith; but again the scripture came into my mind, *'Give and it will be given to you.'*[8] I am here to give and that is what I will do, I determined. So I made a decision that I would not allow my own personal healing need to dominate my thinking. I would pray and make my faith declarations every morning and every night but the rest of my time would be given to the ministry.

With my faith buoyant and a peace in my heart, I began to apply myself to preparation for the task ahead. It is not my practice to travel alone in ministry, and I was to be joined by my colleague David, who was coming by car from Germany and was expected the following day. This would be good, I would have his prayer support, and another thought flashed into my mind; if my lump became worse David could take over the ministry and I could fly home. 'That's not faith!' I reasoned as I tried to push it out of my mind.

The first meeting went well. There was a good crowd and they were very responsive to the Word. I was not allowing my thoughts to stray into forbidden territory. It was good to be in action! When I arrived back at the home of the pastor where I was staying there was a phone call for me. It was David on the line from Germany to say that there was a family emergency which was calling him immediately back to England. My non-faith escape route was gone!

The following day was a real struggle. During the afternoon session I felt weak and ill; it seemed there were aches and pains all over my body, and at times the only thing that kept me upright was hanging onto the pulpit. In the interval between the afternoon and evening meetings I sat in the vestry and cried out to God. The battle was intensifying, the devil was throwing his worst at me. What did I believe, the symptoms or the Word of God? Who was going to have the last word in my life?

As the evening meeting began, I did not feel a great deal better; I had sat down for most of the worship time, which was most unusual. When it was time for the preaching, I climbed wearily behind the pulpit and began to teach the Word. No-one would have guessed the struggle, as I sought to continue as if everything was normal. But then I noticed that something was happening. The longer I preached the stronger I became. I was not preaching on healing; in fact my subject was about the victory of Jesus over all the power of the enemy – Spiritual Warfare. By the end of that evening I could sense that I was on the way towards my personal physical victory.

In one way I was glad to be without David, because it

made it easier to speak my faith declaration and healing scriptures out loud. I continued with the commitment that I had made to God, to pray morning and night for my healing and to give myself the rest of the time unstintingly to the ministry. As the days went by I thought less and less of my own personal need and became fully immersed in the work.

Then one day; was I imagining it or was it really happening? Yes, the lump was getting smaller, or I thought it was. Over the next few days I checked very carefully; something was happening. By the time I returned home an improvement had certainly begun. At last I was able to tell Joyce the whole story and recount my faith battle of the previous weeks. We both agreed that I should be examined by the doctor, which inevitably led to a series of tests at the local hospital. By the time the consultant came to examine me there was no lump left! Hallelujah! All the subsequent tests confirmed that I was in full health, with no cancer in my body.

I was learning that, in a faith battle, it is very important to know who has the last word. Is it God? Or is it fear, doubt, discouragement or even the doctor's gloomy prognosis? Because the last word is where you will be putting your faith. If your confidence is not resting in the mighty power of God, you will be subject to all kinds of fear, which will open the door to the activity of the enemy.

You need to be aware of the strategy of the devil. Jesus said, *'The thief comes only to steal, and kill and destroy.'*[9] The devil's work will always be consistent with his nature. He wants to steal your peace, your health, your future; to destroy your joys, hopes and your family. Jesus declares, *'I have come that they might have life, and have it to the full.'*[10]

Joshua was able to say at the end of his life, *'You know with all your heart and soul that not one of all the good promises the Lord your God gave you has failed. Every promise has been fulfilled; not one has failed.'*[11]

Paul writes to the Corinthians, *'For no matter how many promises God has made, they are "Yes" in Christ.'*[12]

When you take hold of the promises of God, place your full confidence and trust in them, speaking out the Word and making it your constant confession, the last word in your life, you can be confident that God is faithful, and He will do *'immeasurably more than all we ask or imagine, according to his power that is at work within us.'* [13]

Your Health Check-Up

- Whatever your need, who is having the last word in your life?
- Do you know that God's Word is more powerful than all the lies of the devil?
- Is the promise of God giving you a complete victory over fear?
- Are you standing your ground in the face of all symptoms and circumstances?

References

1. Hebrews 10:23
2. Psalm 118:17
3. Psalm 128:4–6
4. Proverbs 4:20–22
5. Exodus 23:25
6. Psalm 30:9
7. Psalm 119:175
8. Luke 6:38
9. John 10:10
10. John 10:10
11. Joshua 23:14
12. 2 Corinthians 1:20
13. Ephesians 3:20

Chapter 11

Have you Drawn a Line on the Past?

Draw a Line on your Family Past

'My mother is deeply involved in witchcraft, my father and uncles are all freemasons, and my whole life is under a cloud of oppression.'

These words, or similar, have been spoken to me on numerous occasions. They pose a very real question in the minds of many people.

'If my parents and ancestors were involved so deeply in the occult and anti-God activity, how can I be free from its effects?'

The direct personal impact on your life through this kind of family involvement will vary greatly, but its lasting effect can be healed and eliminated; for the scripture is clear. *'For you know that it was not with perishable things such as silver or gold that you were redeemed from the empty way of life handed down to you from your forefathers, but with the precious blood of Christ.'* [1] No matter what may be the content of that *'empty way of life'* that was handed down to you from your forefathers, the precious blood of Christ has redeemed you from it.

How this is to be dealt with will vary greatly with each individual. There is no doubt that if your family has had generations of involvement with Satan's kingdom, this may impinge deeply upon you. This may well necessitate a time of prayer and ministry from people with love and experience.

The principles of what happens will not vary, because Jesus on the Cross won a total, irrevocable and eternal victory over all the power of the enemy. The devil is a defeated foe. The instant Jesus rose from the dead, the right of Satan to have any hold on the redeemed children of God ended. Therefore, any hold that the enemy may illegally have put upon you can be broken by the power of the Name of Jesus, and through the victory of His death and resurrection.

Paul when he writes to the church at Colosse makes this abundantly clear; *'God made you alive with Christ. He forgave us all our sins, having cancelled the written code, with its regulations, that was against us and that stood opposed to us; he took it away nailing it to the cross. And having disarmed the powers and authorities, he made a public spectacle of them, triumphing over them by the cross.* [2] We can see here that the authority of the devil, and all his demons has been terminated.

How then are you to know a total and permanent freedom from your negative past? It is by faith. All that we receive from God comes to us through the avenue of faith. *'But without faith it is impossible to please him, for he who comes to God must believe that He is, and that He is the rewarder of those who diligently seek him.'* [3] It may come through the prayers of others, or by your own receiving of the promise in God's Word, but in whatever way it comes, permanent freedom depends on your faith in what God has said and done. The enemy has no right of occupancy in your life.

Let me help you with this practical illustration. When Joyce and I were first married, we lived in a very large house, part of which was our home and part of which was used for the youth work that we were doing. The two areas were clearly defined. It was, therefore, a surprise one evening to arrive home quite late, and find music and laughter coming from our private lounge. I quickly went to enquire from Joyce whether she had invited these young folk to take over our lounge. She had given no such permission and was totally unaware of their presence. I therefore went into action. These young people had no right to be occupying our personal space in our own home. I had a choice: I could ignore their presence, go to bed, and try to get to sleep, despite the noise and disturbance going on below, or exercise my rights and tell them to go. I chose to exercise my rights of ownership and occupancy, walked into the lounge and said, 'The party's over, out you go.' I stood and waited for action, which was instant, as a dozen shame-faced teenagers were ejected, and the door was bolted behind them.

All I did was to exercise my rights. When Jesus becomes the Lord of your life he gives you the right to eject all illegal aliens. Sweep the house clean! Do not forget though to fill it with the power, presence and praises of God. Jesus warned, *'When an evil spirit comes out of a man, it goes through arid places seeking rest and does not find it. Then it says, "I will return to the house I left." When it arrives, it finds the house swept clean and put in order. Then it goes and takes seven other spirits more wicked than itself, and they go in and live there. And the final condition of that man is worse than the first.'*[4]

It is not hard to live in freedom. If your life is submitted to Jesus and you will seek to follow Him, to have fellowship with other believers and to regularly read the Word, pray and worship, then you need not fear re-entry of the negative powers that have dogged your past, because you can draw a line on the past.

Draw a Line on your own Sinful Past

Your problem may not be your family, or your past environment, but your own sins which are dogging your steps. I remember hearing a cassette by Kenneth Hagin, where he gives this testimony. As a young man, Kenneth had an amazing ability to pick locks; this skill became very popular among his mischievous friends. Many times he would be persuaded to open the door of a sweet shop, so that his friends could steal the goods inside. He never stole the sweets himself, but was the necessary accessory before the fact, for without his talent there would be no possibility of the theft at all. Many years passed and Kenneth met with the Lord, was forgiven, transformed and healed by the power of Jesus. In adult life he happened to be back in his home town, talking to some of his childhood friends, when one of them reminded him, 'Do you remember Ken, when you used to pick the lock on the sweet shop over there? Those were the days.'

'No,' said Kenneth, 'that man is dead!'

As the conversation continued, he was able to give testimony to his old friend of the saving power of Jesus and the truth of His Word that says, *'For we know that our old self was crucified with him so that the body of sin might be done away with, that we should no longer be slaves to sin.'*[5] For *'If anyone is in Christ he is a new creation; the old has gone, the new has come!'*[6]

It is essential that you live in the forgiveness of others that is dealt with in Chapter 6, but that forgiveness needs also to be received for your own past, and it is vital to know the truth that on the Cross, *'We were therefore buried with him through baptism into death in order that, just as Christ was raised from the dead through the glory of the Father, we too may live a new life.'*[7]

When we received forgiveness of our sins the Bible says, *'Therefore, since we have been justified through faith, we have peace with God,'*[8] and the meaning of the word justified is, Just–as–if–I'd never sinned. Your past sins may be of a more serious nature than Kenneth Hagin's lock picking, but you still need to know the truth, 'That man is dead,' draw the line, and go forward with Jesus.

Draw a Line on the Painful Past

Incest, sexual abuse, and childhood trauma are incredibly damaging things. The extent of the problem has hit the headlines recently, and shocked the nation. But the good news is that you can live free from the effects of this gross violation of your body and personality, because Jesus is the great healer and restorer.

I have met many people who have experienced such terrible suffering in their childhood. It has brought great shame, guilt and self hatred. The fact that the sin was committed by a close member of the family, in secret, and sometimes with the knowledge of the innocent parent, who failed to intervene, adds to the pain and suffering. This sense of isolation has many times been compounded by the feeling that God doesn't care either. This abuse is not God's fault, but the consequences of sin which has dominated His creation since the fall.

I am glad to say that wonderful healing can come as you receive the understanding that God saw it all along, He agonized with you; and Jesus suffered so that you can be healed. The Psalmist says, *'For you created my inmost being; you knit me together in my mother's womb.'*[9] God saw you before you were born, that is why every embryo is so precious, because God has a purpose for every new life.

The Psalmist continues, *'My frame was not hidden from you when I was made in the secret place. When I was woven together in the depths of the earth, your eyes saw my unformed body. All the days ordained for me were written in your book before one of them came to be.'*[10] God knew you, and saw you, even before you were born, but He is not the author of evil, and His purposes are always good and creative. Jesus said, *'You did not choose me, but I chose you and appointed you to go and bear fruit – fruit that will last.'*[11]

I have seen God bring His healing into many broken and bruised lives, so that marriages have been transformed, families have been united, and lives have been re-created by the power of Jesus. There is a wonderful prophetic scripture in Revelation which, I feel, describes what God does for the broken and abused, *'And I heard a loud voice from the throne saying, "Now the dwelling of God is with men, and he will live with them. They will be his people, and God himself will be with them and be their God. He will wipe every tear from their eyes. There will be no more death or mourning or crying or pain, for the old order of things has passed away." He who was seated on the throne said, "I am making everything new!" Then he said, "Write this down for these words are trust-worthy and true."* [12]

You can go forward, knowing that, because of what Jesus suffered, you are no longer an abused person, but a healed one, who has drawn a line on the shame and suffering, and is walking forward into God's new life.

Draw a Line on Past Failure

Failure, disappointment, discouragement, despair; this is what Joseph must have felt when, having been sold as a slave by his brothers, and just as it seemed his fortunes were improving, he was wrongly accused of trying to rape Potiphar's wife and thrown into jail.

This is what Peter must have felt. Despite having been such a close disciple of Jesus, he lost courage and denied Him three times. The shrill call of the cockerel merely reminded him of the prophetic words of warning spoken by Jesus only hours earlier, as Peter sank into a pit of despair.

This is what Paul must have felt, when the blinding light on the Damascus road knocked him to the ground, sending him reeling, and he heard words from heaven saying, *'Saul, Saul, why do you persecute me?'* [13]

However, Joseph was able to testify to his brothers at the end of his life, after he had seen God redeem his situation and make him the Prime Minister of Egypt, *'You intended to harm me, but God intended it for good to accomplish what is now being done, the saving of many lives.'* [14]

Peter stood on the shores of Galilee, watched Jesus cook him breakfast, and heard Him say, *'Simon son of John, do you love me?'* To which Peter replied, *'Yes, Lord, you know that I love you.'* And three times he heard Jesus re-confirm his calling as the words, *'Feed my lambs, Feed my sheep'*[15] echoed across the waters of Galilee, and Peter knew that he could begin again.

Paul, whilst instructing and directing his young protegé Timothy, gave this testimony, *'I thank Christ Jesus our Lord, who has given me strength, that he considered me faithful, appointing me to his service. Even though I was once a blasphemer and a persecutor and a violent man, I was shown mercy...'*[16]

Paul was perfectly clear concerning right action in dealing with the past, *'But one thing I do: Forgetting what is behind and straining toward what is ahead, I press on toward the goal to win the prize for which God has called me heavenward in Christ Jesus.'*[17]

Amy Carmichael said these words, 'Nothing anyone can do to you can injure you unless you submit to a wrong reaction.' If you have submitted to a wrong reaction in the past, repent of it for the injury can be healed.

There is a great song that has been very popular in my church lately, here are the words –

He whom the Son sets free is free indeed,
Completely liberated from the curse of the law;
He whom the Son sets free is free indeed,
Free to be a servant of the most high God.
For where the Spirit of the Lord is there is liberty,
I am not entangled with the yoke of slavery;
Jesus is the truth that has come to set us free,
I am free, I am free, I am free. [18]

It is a act of faith and obedience to draw a line on the past, declaring that God has dealt with everything sinful or demonic, and that it can have no further hold on you. That faith then needs to take hold of the truth and power of God and to go forward into a life of health, blessing and victory.

Your Health Check-Up

- Have you drawn the line, and been set free from the negative effects of your family's past?
- Have you received forgiveness and drawn the line on your own sinful past?
- Have you received healing for your abused past, and drawn the line that enables you to go forward?
- Have you drawn the line on past failure and disappointment, and are you now walking forward into fruitfulness and blessing?

References

1. 1 Peter 1:18 & 19
2. Colossians 2:13–15
3. Hebrews 11:6 (NKJV)
4. Luke 11:24–26
5. Romans 6:6
6. 2 Corinthians 5:17
7. Romans 6:4
8. Romans 5:1
9. Psalm 139:13
10. Psalm 139:15 & 16
11. John 15:16
12. Revelation 21:3–5
13. Acts 9:4
14. Genesis 50:20
15. John 21:15–17
16. 1 Timothy 1:12 & 13
17. Philippians 3:13 & 14
18. *'He whom the Son sets free,'* by Martin J. Nystrom. Copyright 1991 Integrity's Hosanna! Music. c/o Integrity Music UK Ltd, PO Box 101, Eastbourne, East Sussex, UK BN21 3UX.

Chapter 12

Are you Active or Passive?

It usually takes people by surprise when in the middle of preaching I announce that I am about to do a scientific experiment. I take a pencil out of my pocket and hold it in my right hand. 'Can you see this pencil that I am holding?' I ask, 'Watch very closely because I am about to prove a very important law of physics.' By now many people have already guessed what I am about to do. Yes, I let go of the pencil and it falls to the ground.

'I have just proved that the law of gravity really works,' I triumphantly announce. Some smiles and a few groans is the usual response.

'Now please turn to Romans chapter 8 and verse 2,' is my next request. The curiosity has now been stirred and everyone is waiting to hear what follows.

It says here, *'The law of the spirit of life in Christ Jesus has made me free from the law of sin and death.'*[1] It is very important to understand how these two laws work, and it will be helpful to continue the physics lesson.

When an aircraft is taking on passengers and cargo at the airport, it does not need to be anchored to the ground. The law of gravity is in operation and the plane rests safely on the tarmac. A large modern aircraft can weigh hundreds of tons, and it is a constant marvel that it can soar into the air with such ease and grace. Something very amazing happens at the point of take-off. A higher law comes into operation, which is stronger than the law of gravity. It is the law of flight, and it only occurs because the power of the engines pushes the aircraft through the air at a sufficient speed for its aerodynamic shape to overcome gravity and enable it to fly.

Forts are built on hills because the fighter on the higher ground has – literally! – the upper hand. God has placed a power in our lives that can lift us up onto that higher ground above the law of sin and death that dominates all mankind. It is the power of the Holy Spirit. First, He gives us eternal life and sets us free from judgement and death, but He also gives us a new dimension to our daily living here on earth. His power makes available resources that can release God into every part of our lives and free us from defeat, fear, bondage and sickness. It does not work automatically, but requires faith and obedience on our part.

Let's go back to our air flight. Our aircraft has now taken off and is heading toward its destination with speed and efficiency. The pilot is very pleased with progress so far. However, what if he now decides it is time for a rest and announces to his co-pilot that he will switch off the engines and go back into the passenger cabin for a cup of tea? Once the power has been turned off the plane will lose height and eventually crash to the ground. Why is that? Simply, the law of gravity has not been eliminated, otherwise the plane would already have headed off into outer space. But gravity has been counteracted and overcome by a greater force.

Paul says, *'Live by the Spirit, and you will not gratify the desires of the sinful nature.'*[2] If you will live in the power that God has made available, by remaining on that higher ground, you will be able to receive all the good things that He longs to give to you. Living in the power of the Holy Spirit is not difficult, but it does require active faith.

Diligence is a key word. The writer to the Hebrews says, *'We want each of you to show the same diligence to the very end, in order to make your hope sure. We do not want you to become lazy, but to imitate those who through faith and patience inherit what has been promised.'*[3]

Passivity says, 'It's all up to God.' But God says, 'You do your part, and I will do My part.' Faith needs to be active. We do not live in a world that is bland and devoid of spiritual forces. God is active and all powerful, but Satan is also active and powerful. The good news is that God's power is the greater and that His power lives in you. *'Because the one who is in you is greater than the one who is in the world.'*[4]

However, if you do not use the power that has been given to you, the enemy will quickly step in and rob you of the good things that God wants you to possess. Think back to our illustration; once the plane is in the air the pilot could think that he was doing very well, turn off the power and sit back. The potential outcome is horrific.

Faith is active. The battle is never over until the victory has been won. *Help Yourself to Health* is a way of life, not simply a technique to get your prayers answered.

I am a great fan of the writings of A.W. Tozer. Recently I came across this: 'Everything that is attributed to faith might with equal truth be attributed to prayer, for faith and true prayer are like two sides of the same coin. They are inseparable.' He continues, 'Whatever God can do faith can do, and whatever faith can do prayer can do when it is offered in faith. According to the Bible, we have because we ask, or we have not because we ask not. It does not take much wisdom to discover our next move. Is it not to pray, and pray again and again until the answer comes? God waits to be invited to display His power in behalf of His people.'[5]

Paul writes, *'Since we live by the Spirit, let us keep in step with the Spirit.'*[6] I am teaching you truths that need to become a part of you, deeply ingrained in you through daily practice and constant vigilance, always repelling the attacks of Satan.

Being active in faith does not end there, but needs to continue in every area of your life. Your thinking needs to be renewed by the power of the Word. Your speaking needs to be in line with what God says about you and with the promises of the Bible. You need to live in forgiveness and thanksgiving, and remember, you always have a choice. Choose faith and it will be the keel that keeps your ship upright against every wind that tries to buffet you. As one who 'lives to give' you will always be wanting to *'look not only to your own interests, but also to the interests of others.'*[7]

This kind of living may be very unusual in our sinful and negative world today, but it is the most joyful and full way to live. So help yourself to health, and have a great life enjoying all the blessing, health and prosperity of God.

Your Health Check-Up

- Have you allowed discouragement to make you passive?
- Are you taking steps to renew your mind so that you live in active daily faith?
- Do you want to change your old patterns of living?
- Are you prepared for the active and vigilant attitudes that are needed?

References

1. Romans 8:2 (NKJV)
2. Galatians 5:16
3. Hebrews 6:12
4. 1 John 4:4
5. A.W. Tozer: *The Set of the Sail*, pp. 31 & 32. Publisher: STL and Kingsway
6. Galatians 5:25
7. Philippians 2:4

How to obtain the Bible Plans and Cassette Set referred to in Chapter 8

The Workman's Bible Reading Plan

by Charles Sibthorpe

These are published as two Compact Booklets to give a Simple and Systematic way of Reading through the Bible in **One** or **Two** Years

One Year Plan – Each day a chapter is read from the Psalms or Proverbs, a chapter from the New Testament and two from the Old Testament. The selection has been carefully made to make each day's portion stimulating and balanced. The Psalms, Proverbs and Gospels are read twice each year, the rest of the Bible once. It takes approximately 20 minutes each day.

Two Year Plan – The New Testament, Psalms and Proverbs are read each year, together with one half of the Old Testament. This will take you approximately 12–15 minutes each day.

Each Booklet costs £1.00 including postage, and can be purchased from the address on the next page.

Developing Spiritual Sensitivity

by Joyce Sibthorpe

This teaching is contained in a Two Cassette Set and gives clear and anointed teaching on:
– How to hear the voice of God, and
– How to develop a strong and meaningful time with God each day.

This teaching was given at the Faith Camp some years ago and has provided help to many hundreds of people.

The Cassette Set costs £6.00 including postage, and can be purchased from:

> 222 Publications
> 71 High Street
> Nailsea
> Bristol BS19 1AW
>
> Telephone and Fax (0275) 855988